CS-40　GENERAL APTITUDE AND ABILITIES SERIES

*This is your*
*PASSBOOK for...*

# Interviewing

*Test Preparation Study Guide*
*Questions & Answers*

**NATIONAL LEARNING CORPORATION** ®

# COPYRIGHT NOTICE

This book is SOLELY intended for, is sold ONLY to, and its use is RESTRICTED to individual, bona fide applicants or candidates who qualify by virtue of having seriously filed applications for appropriate license, certificate, professional and/or promotional advancement, higher school matriculation, scholarship, or other legitimate requirements of education and/or governmental authorities.

This book is NOT intended for use, class instruction, tutoring, training, duplication, copying, reprinting, excerption, or adaptation, etc., by:

1) Other publishers
2) Proprietors and/or Instructors of "Coaching" and/or Preparatory Courses
3) Personnel and/or Training Divisions of commercial, industrial, and governmental organizations
4) Schools, colleges, or universities and/or their departments and staffs, including teachers and other personnel
5) Testing Agencies or Bureaus
6) Study groups which seek by the purchase of a single volume to copy and/or duplicate and/or adapt this material for use by the group as a whole without having purchased individual volumes for each of the members of the group
7) Et al.

Such persons would be in violation of appropriate Federal and State statutes.

PROVISION OF LICENSING AGREEMENTS – Recognized educational, commercial, industrial, and governmental institutions and organizations, and others legitimately engaged in educational pursuits, including training, testing, and measurement activities, may address request for a licensing agreement to the copyright owners, who will determine whether, and under what conditions, including fees and charges, the materials in this book may be used them.  In other words, a licensing facility exists for the legitimate use of the material in this book on other than an individual basis.  However, it is asseverated and affirmed here that the material in this book CANNOT be used without the receipt of the express permission of such a licensing agreement from the Publishers. Inquiries re licensing should be addressed to the company, attention rights and permissions department.

All rights reserved, including the right of reproduction in whole or in part, in any form or by any means, electronic or mechanical, including photocopying, recording, or by any information storage and retrieval system, without permission in writing from the Publisher.

Copyright © 2025 by
## National Learning Corporation

212 Michael Drive, Syosset, NY 11791
(516) 921-8888 • www.passbooks.com
E-mail: info@passbooks.com

# PASSBOOK® SERIES

THE *PASSBOOK® SERIES* has been created to prepare applicants and candidates for the ultimate academic battlefield – the examination room.

At some time in our lives, each and every one of us may be required to take an examination – for validation, matriculation, admission, qualification, registration, certification, or licensure.

Based on the assumption that every applicant or candidate has met the basic formal educational standards, has taken the required number of courses, and read the necessary texts, the *PASSBOOK® SERIES* furnishes the one special preparation which may assure passing with confidence, instead of failing with insecurity. Examination questions – together with answers – are furnished as the basic vehicle for study so that the mysteries of the examination and its compounding difficulties may be eliminated or diminished by a sure method.

This book is meant to help you pass your examination provided that you qualify and are serious in your objective.

The entire field is reviewed through the huge store of content information which is succinctly presented through a provocative and challenging approach – the question-and-answer method.

A climate of success is established by furnishing the correct answers at the end of each test.

You soon learn to recognize types of questions, forms of questions, and patterns of questioning. You may even begin to anticipate expected outcomes.

You perceive that many questions are repeated or adapted so that you can gain acute insights, which may enable you to score many sure points.

You learn how to confront new questions, or types of questions, and to attack them confidently and work out the correct answers.

You note objectives and emphases, and recognize pitfalls and dangers, so that you may make positive educational adjustments.

Moreover, you are kept fully informed in relation to new concepts, methods, practices, and directions in the field.

You discover that you are actually taking the examination all the time: you are preparing for the examination by "taking" an examination, not by reading extraneous and/or supererogatory textbooks.

In short, this PASSBOOK®, used directedly, should be an important factor in helping you to pass your test.

# INTERVIEWING

The General Aptitude and Abilities Series provides functional, intensive test practice and drill in the basic skills and areas common to many civil service, general aptitude and achievement examinations necessary for entrance into schools or occupations.

Passbooks in this series use a variety of question types, and other applicable items like charts, graphs, illustrations and more, to prepare candidates for testing in particular subject areas. This Passbook features a wide range of questions covering fundamentals of interviewing; and more.

# HOW TO TAKE A TEST

You have studied long, hard and conscientiously.

With your official admission card in hand, and your heart pounding, you have been admitted to the examination room.

You note that there are several hundred other applicants in the examination room waiting to take the same test.

They all appear to be equally well prepared.

You know that nothing but your best effort will suffice. The "moment of truth" is at hand: you now have to demonstrate objectively, in writing, your knowledge of content and your understanding of subject matter.

You are fighting the most important battle of your life—to pass and/or score high on an examination which will determine your career and provide the economic basis for your livelihood.

What extra, special things should you know and should you do in taking the examination?

I. YOU MUST PASS AN EXAMINATION

A. WHAT EVERY CANDIDATE SHOULD KNOW
Examination applicants often ask us for help in preparing for the written test. What can I study in advance? What kinds of questions will be asked? How will the test be given? How will the papers be graded?

B. HOW ARE EXAMS DEVELOPED?
Examinations are carefully written by trained technicians who are specialists in the field known as "psychological measurement," in consultation with recognized authorities in the field of work that the test will cover. These experts recommend the subject matter areas or skills to be tested; only those knowledges or skills important to your success on the job are included. The most reliable books and source materials available are used as references. Together, the experts and technicians judge the difficulty level of the questions.
Test technicians know how to phrase questions so that the problem is clearly stated. Their ethics do not permit "trick" or "catch" questions. Questions may have been tried out on sample groups, or subjected to statistical analysis, to determine their usefulness.
Written tests are often used in combination with performance tests, ratings of training and experience, and oral interviews. All of these measures combine to form the best-known means of finding the right person for the right job.

## II. HOW TO PASS THE WRITTEN TEST

### A. BASIC STEPS

1) Study the announcement

How, then, can you know what subjects to study? Our best answer is: "Learn as much as possible about the class of positions for which you've applied." The exam will test the knowledge, skills and abilities needed to do the work.

Your most valuable source of information about the position you want is the official exam announcement. This announcement lists the training and experience qualifications. Check these standards and apply only if you come reasonably close to meeting them. Many jurisdictions preview the written test in the exam announcement by including a section called "Knowledge and Abilities Required," "Scope of the Examination," or some similar heading. Here you will find out specifically what fields will be tested.

2) Choose appropriate study materials

If the position for which you are applying is technical or advanced, you will read more advanced, specialized material. If you are already familiar with the basic principles of your field, elementary textbooks would waste your time. Concentrate on advanced textbooks and technical periodicals. Think through the concepts and review difficult problems in your field.

These are all general sources. You can get more ideas on your own initiative, following these leads. For example, training manuals and publications of the government agency which employs workers in your field can be useful, particularly for technical and professional positions. A letter or visit to the government department involved may result in more specific study suggestions, and certainly will provide you with a more definite idea of the exact nature of the position you are seeking.

3) Study this book!

## III. KINDS OF TESTS

Tests are used for purposes other than measuring knowledge and ability to perform specified duties. For some positions, it is equally important to test ability to make adjustments to new situations or to profit from training. In others, basic mental abilities not dependent on information are essential. Questions which test these things may not appear as pertinent to the duties of the position as those which test for knowledge and information. Yet they are often highly important parts of a fair examination. For very general questions, it is almost impossible to help you direct your study efforts. What we can do is to point out some of the more common of these general abilities needed in public service positions and describe some typical questions.

1) General information

Broad, general information has been found useful for predicting job success in some kinds of work. This is tested in a variety of ways, from vocabulary lists to questions about current events. Basic background in some field of work, such as sociology or economics, may be sampled in a group of questions. Often these are principles which have become familiar to most persons through exposure rather than through formal training. It is difficult to advise you how to study for these questions; being alert to the world around you is our best suggestion.

2) Verbal ability

An example of an ability needed in many positions is verbal or language ability. Verbal ability is, in brief, the ability to use and understand words. Vocabulary and grammar tests are typical measures of this ability. Reading comprehension or paragraph interpretation questions are common in many kinds of civil service tests. You are given a paragraph of written material and asked to find its central meaning.

## IV. KINDS OF QUESTIONS

1. Multiple-choice Questions

Most popular of the short-answer questions is the "multiple choice" or "best answer" question. It can be used, for example, to test for factual knowledge, ability to solve problems or judgment in meeting situations found at work.

A multiple-choice question is normally one of three types:
- It can begin with an incomplete statement followed by several possible endings. You are to find the one ending which best completes the statement, although some of the others may not be entirely wrong.
- It can also be a complete statement in the form of a question which is answered by choosing one of the statements listed.
- It can be in the form of a problem – again you select the best answer.

Here is an example of a multiple-choice question with a discussion which should give you some clues as to the method for choosing the right answer:

When an employee has a complaint about his assignment, the action which will best help him overcome his difficulty is to
    A. discuss his difficulty with his coworkers
    B. take the problem to the head of the organization
    C. take the problem to the person who gave him the assignment
    D. say nothing to anyone about his complaint

In answering this question, you should study each of the choices to find which is best. Consider choice "A" – Certainly an employee may discuss his complaint with fellow employees, but no change or improvement can result, and the complaint remains unresolved. Choice "B" is a poor choice since the head of the organization probably does not know what assignment you have been given, and taking your problem to him is known as "going over the head" of the supervisor. The supervisor, or person who made the assignment, is the person who can clarify it or correct any injustice. Choice "C" is, therefore, correct. To say nothing, as in choice "D," is unwise. Supervisors have and interest in knowing the problems employees are facing, and the employee is seeking a solution to his problem.

2. True/False

3. Matching Questions

Matching an answer from a column of choices within another column.

## V. RECORDING YOUR ANSWERS

Computer terminals are used more and more today for many different kinds of exams.

For an examination with very few applicants, you may be told to record your answers in the test booklet itself. Separate answer sheets are much more common. If this separate answer sheet is to be scored by machine – and this is often the case – it is highly important that you mark your answers correctly in order to get credit.

## VI. BEFORE THE TEST

**YOUR PHYSICAL CONDITION IS IMPORTANT**

If you are not well, you can't do your best work on tests. If you are half asleep, you can't do your best either. Here are some tips:

1) Get about the same amount of sleep you usually get. Don't stay up all night before the test, either partying or worrying—DON'T DO IT!
2) If you wear glasses, be sure to wear them when you go to take the test. This goes for hearing aids, too.
3) If you have any physical problems that may keep you from doing your best, be sure to tell the person giving the test. If you are sick or in poor health, you relay cannot do your best on any test. You can always come back and take the test some other time.

Common sense will help you find procedures to follow to get ready for an examination. Too many of us, however, overlook these sensible measures. Indeed, nervousness and fatigue have been found to be the most serious reasons why applicants fail to do their best on civil service tests. Here is a list of reminders:

- Begin your preparation early – Don't wait until the last minute to go scurrying around for books and materials or to find out what the position is all about.
- Prepare continuously – An hour a night for a week is better than an all-night cram session. This has been definitely established. What is more, a night a week for a month will return better dividends than crowding your study into a shorter period of time.
- Locate the place of the exam – You have been sent a notice telling you when and where to report for the examination. If the location is in a different town or otherwise unfamiliar to you, it would be well to inquire the best route and learn something about the building.
- Relax the night before the test – Allow your mind to rest. Do not study at all that night. Plan some mild recreation or diversion; then go to bed early and get a good night's sleep.
- Get up early enough to make a leisurely trip to the place for the test – This way unforeseen events, traffic snarls, unfamiliar buildings, etc. will not upset you.
- Dress comfortably – A written test is not a fashion show. You will be known by number and not by name, so wear something comfortable.
- Leave excess paraphernalia at home – Shopping bags and odd bundles will get in your way. You need bring only the items mentioned in the official notice you received; usually everything you need is provided. Do not bring reference books to the exam. They will only confuse those last minutes and be taken away from you when in the test room.

- Arrive somewhat ahead of time – If because of transportation schedules you must get there very early, bring a newspaper or magazine to take your mind off yourself while waiting.
- Locate the examination room – When you have found the proper room, you will be directed to the seat or part of the room where you will sit. Sometimes you are given a sheet of instructions to read while you are waiting. Do not fill out any forms until you are told to do so; just read them and be prepared.
- Relax and prepare to listen to the instructions
- If you have any physical problem that may keep you from doing your best, be sure to tell the test administrator. If you are sick or in poor health, you really cannot do your best on the exam. You can come back and take the test some other time.

## VII. AT THE TEST

The day of the test is here and you have the test booklet in your hand. The temptation to get going is very strong. Caution! There is more to success than knowing the right answers. You must know how to identify your papers and understand variations in the type of short-answer question used in this particular examination. Follow these suggestions for maximum results from your efforts:

1) Cooperate with the monitor

The test administrator has a duty to create a situation in which you can be as much at ease as possible. He will give instructions, tell you when to begin, check to see that you are marking your answer sheet correctly, and so on. He is not there to guard you, although he will see that your competitors do not take unfair advantage. He wants to help you do your best.

2) Listen to all instructions

Don't jump the gun! Wait until you understand all directions. In most civil service tests you get more time than you need to answer the questions. So don't be in a hurry. Read each word of instructions until you clearly understand the meaning. Study the examples, listen to all announcements and follow directions. Ask questions if you do not understand what to do.

3) Identify your papers

Civil service exams are usually identified by number only. You will be assigned a number; you must not put your name on your test papers. Be sure to copy your number correctly. Since more than one exam may be given, copy your exact examination title.

4) Plan your time

Unless you are told that a test is a "speed" or "rate of work" test, speed itself is usually not important. Time enough to answer all the questions will be provided, but this does not mean that you have all day. An overall time limit has been set. Divide the total time (in minutes) by the number of questions to determine the approximate time you have for each question.

5) Do not linger over difficult questions

If you come across a difficult question, mark it with a paper clip (useful to have along) and come back to it when you have been through the booklet. One caution if you do this – be sure to skip a number on your answer sheet as well. Check often to be sure that you have not lost your place and that you are marking in the row numbered the same as the question you are answering.

6) Read the questions
Be sure you know what the question asks! Many capable people are unsuccessful because they failed to read the questions correctly.

7) Answer all questions
Unless you have been instructed that a penalty will be deducted for incorrect answers, it is better to guess than to omit a question.

8) Speed tests
It is often better NOT to guess on speed tests. It has been found that on timed tests people are tempted to spend the last few seconds before time is called in marking answers at random – without even reading them – in the hope of picking up a few extra points. To discourage this practice, the instructions may warn you that your score will be "corrected" for guessing. That is, a penalty will be applied. The incorrect answers will be deducted from the correct ones, or some other penalty formula will be used.

9) Review your answers
If you finish before time is called, go back to the questions you guessed or omitted to give them further thought. Review other answers if you have time.

10) Return your test materials
If you are ready to leave before others have finished or time is called, take ALL your materials to the monitor and leave quietly. Never take any test material with you. The monitor can discover whose papers are not complete, and taking a test booklet may be grounds for disqualification.

VIII. EXAMINATION TECHNIQUES

1) Read the general instructions carefully. These are usually printed on the first page of the exam booklet. As a rule, these instructions refer to the timing of the examination; the fact that you should not start work until the signal and must stop work at a signal, etc. If there are any special instructions, such as a choice of questions to be answered, make sure that you note this instruction carefully.

2) When you are ready to start work on the examination, that is as soon as the signal has been given, read the instructions to each question booklet, underline any key words or phrases, such as least, best, outline, describe and the like. In this way you will tend to answer as requested rather than discover on reviewing your paper that you listed without describing, that you selected the worst choice rather than the best choice, etc.

3) If the examination is of the objective or multiple-choice type – that is, each question will also give a series of possible answers: A, B, C or D, and you are called upon to select the best answer and write the letter next to that answer on your answer paper – it is advisable to start answering each question in turn. There may be anywhere from 50 to 100 such questions in the three or four hours allotted and you can see how much time would be taken if you read through all the questions before beginning to answer any. Furthermore, if you

come across a question or group of questions which you know would be difficult to answer, it would undoubtedly affect your handling of all the other questions.

4) If the examination is of the essay type and contains but a few questions, it is a moot point as to whether you should read all the questions before starting to answer any one. Of course, if you are given a choice – say five out of seven and the like – then it is essential to read all the questions so you can eliminate the two that are most difficult. If, however, you are asked to answer all the questions, there may be danger in trying to answer the easiest one first because you may find that you will spend too much time on it. The best technique is to answer the first question, then proceed to the second, etc.

5) Time your answers. Before the exam begins, write down the time it started, then add the time allowed for the examination and write down the time it must be completed, then divide the time available somewhat as follows:
    - If 3-1/2 hours are allowed, that would be 210 minutes. If you have 80 objective-type questions, that would be an average of 2-1/2 minutes per question. Allow yourself no more than 2 minutes per question, or a total of 160 minutes, which will permit about 50 minutes to review.
    - If for the time allotment of 210 minutes there are 7 essay questions to answer, that would average about 30 minutes a question. Give yourself only 25 minutes per question so that you have about 35 minutes to review.

6) The most important instruction is to read each question and make sure you know what is wanted. The second most important instruction is to time yourself properly so that you answer every question. The third most important instruction is to answer every question. Guess if you have to but include something for each question. Remember that you will receive no credit for a blank and will probably receive some credit if you write something in answer to an essay question. If you guess a letter – say "B" for a multiple-choice question – you may have guessed right. If you leave a blank as an answer to a multiple-choice question, the examiners may respect your feelings but it will not add a point to your score. Some exams may penalize you for wrong answers, so in such cases only, you may not want to guess unless you have some basis for your answer.

7) Suggestions
    a. Objective-type questions
        1. Examine the question booklet for proper sequence of pages and questions
        2. Read all instructions carefully
        3. Skip any question which seems too difficult; return to it after all other questions have been answered
        4. Apportion your time properly; do not spend too much time on any single question or group of questions
        5. Note and underline key words – all, most, fewest, least, best, worst, same, opposite, etc.
        6. Pay particular attention to negatives
        7. Note unusual option, e.g., unduly long, short, complex, different or similar in content to the body of the question
        8. Observe the use of "hedging" words – probably, may, most likely, etc.

9. Make sure that your answer is put next to the same number as the question
10. Do not second-guess unless you have good reason to believe the second answer is definitely more correct
11. Cross out original answer if you decide another answer is more accurate; do not erase until you are ready to hand your paper in
12. Answer all questions; guess unless instructed otherwise
13. Leave time for review

b. Essay questions
1. Read each question carefully
2. Determine exactly what is wanted. Underline key words or phrases.
3. Decide on outline or paragraph answer
4. Include many different points and elements unless asked to develop any one or two points or elements
5. Show impartiality by giving pros and cons unless directed to select one side only
6. Make and write down any assumptions you find necessary to answer the questions
7. Watch your English, grammar, punctuation and choice of words
8. Time your answers; don't crowd material

8) Answering the essay question

Most essay questions can be answered by framing the specific response around several key words or ideas. Here are a few such key words or ideas:

M's: manpower, materials, methods, money, management
P's: purpose, program, policy, plan, procedure, practice, problems, pitfalls, personnel, public relations

a. Six basic steps in handling problems:
1. Preliminary plan and background development
2. Collect information, data and facts
3. Analyze and interpret information, data and facts
4. Analyze and develop solutions as well as make recommendations
5. Prepare report and sell recommendations
6. Install recommendations and follow up effectiveness

b. Pitfalls to avoid
1. Taking things for granted – A statement of the situation does not necessarily imply that each of the elements is necessarily true; for example, a complaint may be invalid and biased so that all that can be taken for granted is that a complaint has been registered
2. Considering only one side of a situation – Wherever possible, indicate several alternatives and then point out the reasons you selected the best one
3. Failing to indicate follow up – Whenever your answer indicates action on your part, make certain that you will take proper follow-up action to see how successful your recommendations, procedures or actions turn out to be
4. Taking too long in answering any single question – Remember to time your answers properly

# EXAMINATION SECTION

# INTERVIEWING
# EXAMINATION SECTION
# TEST 1

DIRECTIONS: Each question or incomplete statement is followed by several suggested answers or completions. Select the one that BEST answers the question or completes the statement. *PRINT THE LETTER OF THE CORRECT ANSWER IN THE SPACE AT THE RIGHT.*

1. Of the methods given below for obtaining desired information from applicants, the one considered the BEST interviewing method is to
   A. work from an outline, asking the questions in the order in which they appear and requiring the applicant to give specific answers
   B. let the applicant tell what he has to say in his own way first, the interviewer then taking responsibility for asking questions on points not covered
   C. tell the applicant all the facts that it is necessary to have, then letting him give the information in any way he chooses
   D. verify all such facts as birth date, income, and past employment before seeing the applicant, then asking the applicant to fill in the remaining gaps when he is interviewed

1.____

2. Suppose an applicant objects to answering a question regarding his recent employment and asks, "What business is it of yours, young man?"
   In conducting the interview, the MOST constructive course of action for you to take under the circumstances would be to
   A. tell the applicant you have no intention of prying into his personal affairs and go on to the next question
   B. refer the applicant to your supervisor
   C. rephrase the question so that only a "Yes" or "No" answer is required
   D. explain why the question is being asked

2.____

3. An interview is BEST conducted in private PRIMARILY because
   A. the person interviewed will tend to be less self-conscious
   B. the interviewer will be able to maintain his continuity of thought better
   C. it will insure that the interview is "off the record"
   D. people tend to "show off" before an audience

3.____

4. An interviewer will be better able to understand the person interviewed and his problems if he recognizes that much of the person's behavior is due to motives
   A. which are deliberate           B. of which he is unaware
   C. which are inexplicable         D. which are kept under control

4.____

5. When an applicant is repeatedly told that "everything will be all right," the effect that can USUALLY be expected is that he will
   A. develop overt negativistic reactions toward the agency
   B. become too closely identified with the interviewer
   C. doubt the interviewer's ability to understand and help with his problems
   D. have greater confidence in the interviewer

6. While interviewing a client, it is PREFERABLE that the interviewer
   A. take no notes in order to avoid disturbing the client
   B. focus primary attention on the client while the client is talking
   C. take no notes in order to impress upon the client the interviewer's ability to remember all the pertinent facts of his case
   D. record all the details in order to show the client that what he says is important

7. During an interview, a curious applicant asks several questions about the interviewer's private life.
   As the interviewer, you should
   A. refuse to answer such questions
   B. answer his questions fully
   C. explain that your primary concern is with his problems and that discussion of your personal affairs will not be helpful in meeting his needs
   D. explain that it is the responsibility of the interviewer to ask questions and not to answer them

8. An interviewer can BEST establish a good relationship with the person being interviewed by
   A. assuming casual interest in the statements made by the person being interviewed
   B. asking questions which enable the person to show pride in his knowledge
   C. taking the point of view of the person interviewed
   D. showing a genuine interest in the person

9. An interviewer's attention must be directed toward himself as well as toward the person interviewed.
   This statement means that the interviewer should
   A. keep in mind the extent to which his own prejudices may influence his judgment
   B. rationalize the statements made by the person interviewed
   C. gain the respect and confidence of the person interviewed
   D. avoid being too impersonal

10. More complete expression will be obtained from a person being interviewed if the interviewer can create the impression that
    A. the data secured will become part of a permanent record
    B. official information must be accurate in every detail
    C. it is the duty of the person interviewed to give accurate data
    D. the person interviewed is participating in a discussion of his own problems

11. The practice of asking leading questions should be avoided in an interview because the
    A. interviewer risks revealing his attitudes to the person being interviewed
    B. interviewer may be led to ignore the objective attitudes of the person interviewed
    C. answers may be unwarrantedly influenced
    D. person interviewed will resent the attempt to lead him and will be less cooperative

11.____

12. A good technique for the interviewer to use in an effort to secure reliable data and to reduce the possibility of misunderstanding is to
    A. use casual undirected conversation, enabling the person being interviewed to talk about himself, and thus secure the desired information
    B. adopt the procedure of using direct questions regularly
    C. extract the desired information from the person being interviewed by putting him on the defensive
    D. explain to the person being interviewed the information desired and the reason for needing it

12.____

13. In interviewing an applicant, your attitude toward his veracity should be that the information he has furnished you is
    A. *untruthful* until you have had an opportunity to check the information
    B. *truthful* only insofar as verifiable facts are concerned
    C. *untruthful* because clients tend to interpret everything in their own favor
    D. *truthful* until you have information to the contrary

13.____

14. When an agency assigns its most experienced interviewers to conduct initial interviews with applicants, the MOST important reason for its action is that
    A. experienced workers are always older and, therefore, command the respect of applicants
    B. the applicant may be given a complete understanding of the procedures to be followed and the time involved in obtaining assistance
    C. applicants with fraudulent intentions will be detected, and prevented from obtaining further services from the agency
    D. the applicant may be given an understanding of the purpose of the assistance program and of the bases for granting assistance, in addition to the routine information

14.____

15. In conducting the first interview with an applicant, you should
    A. ask questions requiring "Yes" or "No" answers in order to simplify the interview
    B. rephrase several of the key questions as a check on his previous statements
    C. let him tell his own story while keeping him to the relevant facts
    D. avoid showing any sympathy for the applicant while he is revealing his personal needs and problems

15.____

16. When an interview opens an interview by asking the client direct questions about his work, it is very likely that the client will feel
    A. that the interview is interested in him
    B. at ease if his work has been good
    C. free to discuss his attitudes toward his work
    D. that good reports are of great importance to the interviewer in his thinking

16.____

17. When an interviewer does NOT understand the meaning of a response that a client has made, the interviewer should
    A. proceed to another topic
    B. state that he does not understand and ask for clarification
    C. act as if he understands so that the client's confidence in him should not be shaken
    D. ask the client to rephrase his response

17.____

18. When an interviewer makes a response which brings on a high degree of resistance in the client, he should
    A. apologize and rephrase his remark in a less evocative manner
    B. accept the resistance on the part of the client
    C. ignore the client's resistance
    D. recognize that little more will be accomplished in the interview and suggest another appointment

18.____

19. Most definitions of interviewing would NOT include the following as a necessary aspect:
    A. The interviewer and client meet face-to-face and talk things out
    B. The client is experiencing considerable emotional disturbance
    C. A valuable learning opportunity is provided for the client
    D. The interviewer brings a special competence to the relationship

19.____

20. A powerful dynamic in the interviewing process and often the very *antonym* of its counterpart in the instructional process is
    A. encouraging accuracy
    B. emphasizing structure
    C. pointing up sequential and orderly thinking
    D. processing ambiguity and equivocation

20.____

21. Interviewing techniques are frequently useful in working with clients.
    A basic fundamental is an atmosphere which may BEST be described as
    A. non-threatening
    B. motivating for creativity
    C. highly charged to stimulate excitement
    D. fairly-well structured

21.____

22. In interviewing the disadvantaged client, the subtle technique of steering away from high-level educational and vocational plans must be *replaced* by
    A. a wait-and-see explanation to the client
    B. the use of prediction tables to determine possibilities and probabilities of overcoming this condition

22.____

C. avoidance in discussing controversial issues of deprivation
D. encouragement and concrete consideration for planning his future

23. The process of collecting, analyzing, synthesizing, and interpreting information about the client should be
    A. completed prior to interviewing
    B. completed early in the interviewing process
    C. limited to a type of interviewing which is primarily diagnostic in purpose
    D. continuously pursued throughout interviewing

24. Catharsis, the "emotional unloading" of the client's feelings, has a value in the early stages of interviewing because it accomplishes all BUT which one of the following goals?
    It
    A. relieves strong physiological tensions in the client
    B. increases the client's anxiety and aggrandizes his motivation to continue counseling
    C. provides a strong substitute for "acting out" the client's feelings
    D. releases emotional energy which the client has been using to bulwark his defenses

25. In the interviewing process, the interviewer should *usually* give information
    A. whenever it is needed
    B. at the end of the process
    C. in the introductory interview
    D. just before the client would ordinarily request it

## KEY (CORRECT ANSWERS)

| | | | | |
|---|---|---|---|---|
| 1. | B | | 11. | C |
| 2. | D | | 12. | D |
| 3. | A | | 13. | D |
| 4. | B | | 14. | D |
| 5. | C | | 15. | C |
| 6. | B | | 16. | D |
| 7. | C | | 17. | B |
| 8. | D | | 18. | B |
| 9. | A | | 19. | B |
| 10. | D | | 20. | D |

| | |
|---|---|
| 21. | A |
| 22. | D |
| 23. | D |
| 24. | B |
| 25. | A |

# TEST 2

DIRECTIONS: Each question or incomplete statement is followed by several suggested answers or completions. Select the one that BEST answers the question or completes the statement. *PRINT THE LETTER OF THE CORRECT ANSWER IN THE SPACE AT THE RIGHT.*

1. Of the following problems that might affect the conduct and outcome of an interview, the MOST troublesome and usually the MOST difficult for the interviewer to control is the
    A. tendency of the interviewee to anticipate the needs and preferences of the interviewer
    B. impulse to cut the interviewee off when he seems to have reached the end of an idea
    C. tendency of interviewee attitude to bias the results
    D. tendency of the interviewer to do most of the talking

1.____

2. The supervisor MOST likely to be a good interviewer is one who
    A. is adept at manipulating people and circumstances toward his objective
    B. is able to put himself in the position of the interviewee
    C. gets the more difficult questions out of the way at the beginning of the interview
    D. develops one style and technique that can be used in any type of interview

2.____

3. A good interviewer guards against the tendency to form an overall opinion about an interviewee on the basis of a single aspect of the interviewee's makeup.
   This statement refers to a well-known source of error in interviewing known as the
    A. assumption error        B. expectancy error
    C. extension effect        D. halo effect

3.____

4. In conducting an "exit interview" with an employee who is leaving voluntarily, the interview's MAIN objective should be to
    A. see that the employee leaves with a good opinion of the organization
    B. learn the true reasons for the employee's resignation
    C. find out if the employee would consider a transfer
    D. try to get the employee to remain on the job

4.____

5. During an interview, an interviewee unexpectedly discloses a relevant but embarrassing personal fact.
   It would be BEST for the interviewer to
    A. listen calmly, avoiding any gesture or facial expression that would suggest approval or disapproval of what is related
    B. change the subject, since further discussion in this area may reveal other embarrassing, but irrelevant, personal facts

5.____

C. apologize to the interviewee for having led him to reveal such a fact and promise not to do so again
D. bring the interview to a close as quickly as possible in order to avoid a discussion which may be distressing to the interviewee

6. Suppose that, while you are interviewing an applicant for a position in your office, you notice a contradiction in facts in two of his responses.
For you to call the contradictions to his attention would be
   A. *inadvisable*, because it reduces the interviewee's level of participation
   B. *advisable*, because getting the facts is essential to a successful interview
   C. *inadvisable*, because the interviewer should use more subtle techniques to resolve any discrepancies
   D. *advisable*, because the interviewee should be impressed with the necessity for giving consistent answers

6.____

7. An interviewer should be aware that an undesirable result of including "leading questions" in an interview is to
   A. cause the interviewee to give a "yes" or "no" answers with qualification or explanation
   B. encourage the interviewee to discuss irrelevant topics
   C. encourage the interviewee to give more meaningful information
   D. reduce the validity of the information obtained from the interviewee

7.____

8. The kind of interview which is particularly helpful in getting an employee to tell about his complaints and grievances is one in which
   A. a pattern has been worked out involving a sequence of exact questions to be asked
   B. the interviewee is expected to support his statements with specific evidence
   C. the interviewee is not made to answer specific questions but is encouraged to talk freely
   D. the interviewer has specific items on which he wishes to get or give information

8.____

9. Suppose you are scheduled to interview an employee under your supervision concerning a health problem. You know that some of the questions you will be asking him will seem embarrassing to him, and that he may resist answering these questions.
In general, to hold these questions for the last part of the interview would be
   A. *desirable*; the intervening time period gives the interviewer an opportunity to plan how to ask these sensitive questions.
   B. *undesirable*; the employee will probably feel that he has been tricked when he suddenly must answer embarrassing questions
   C. *desirable*; the employee will probably have increased confidence in the interviewer and be more willing to answer these questions
   D. *undesirable*; questions that are important should not be deferred until the end of the interview

9.____

10. In conducting an interview, the BEST types of questions with which to begin the interview are those which the person interviewed is
    A. willing and able to answer
    B. willing but unable to answer
    C. able but unwilling to answer
    D. unable and unwilling to answer

11. In order to determine accurately a child's age, it is BEST for an interviewer to rely on
    A. the child's grade in school
    B. what the mother says
    C. birth records
    D. a library card

12. In his first interview with a new employee, it would be LEAST appropriate for a unit supervisor to
    A. find out the employee's preference for the several types of jobs to which he is able to assign him
    B. determine whether the employee will make good promotion material
    C. inform the employee of what his basic job responsibilities will be
    D. inquire about the employee's education and previous employment

13. If an interviewer takes care to phrase his questions carefully and precisely, the result will MOST probably be that
    A. he will be able to determine whether the person interviewed is being truthful
    B. the free flow of the interview will be lost
    C. he will get the information he wants
    D. he will ask stereotyped questions and narrow the scope of the interview

14. When, during an interview, is the person interviewed LEAST likely to be cautious about what he tells the interviewer?
    A. Shortly after the beginning when the questions normally suggest pleasant associations to the person interviewed
    B. As long as the interviewer keeps his questions to the point
    C. At the point where the person interviewed gains a clear insight into the area being discussed
    D. When the interview appears formally ended and goodbyes are being said

15. In an interview held for the purpose of getting information from the person interviewed, it is sometimes desirable for the interviewer to repeat the answer he has received to a question.
    For the interviewer to rephrase such an answer in his own words is good practice MAINLY because it
    A. gives the interviewer time to make up his next question
    B. gives the person interviewed a chance to correct any possible misunderstanding
    C. gives the person interviewed the feeling that the interviewer considers his answer important
    D. prevents the person interviewed from changing his answer

16. There are several methods of formulating questions during an interview. The particular method used should be adapted to the interview problems presented by the person being questioned.
    Of the following methods of formulating questions during an interview, the ACCEPTABLE one is for the interviewer to ask questions which
    A. incorporate several items in order to allow a cooperative interviewee freedom to organize his statements
    B. are ambiguous in order to foil a distrustful interviewee
    C. suggest the correct answer in order to assist an interviewee who appears confused
    D. would help an otherwise unresponsive interviewee to become more responsive

16.____

17. For an interviewer to permit the person being interviewed to read the data the interviewer writes as he records the person's responses on a routine departmental form is
    A. *desirable*, because it serves to assure the person interviewed that his responses are being recorded accurately
    B. *undesirable*, because it prevents the interviewer from clarifying uncertain points by asking additional questions
    C. *desirable*, because it makes the time that the person interviewed must wait while the answer is written seem shorter
    D. *undesirable*, because it destroys the confidentiality of the interview

17.____

18. Of the following methods of conducting an interview, the BEST is to
    A. ask questions with "yes" or "no" answers
    B. listen carefully and ask only questions that are pertinent
    C. fire questions at the interviewee so that he must answer sincerely and briefly
    D. read standardized questions to the person being interviewed

18.____

# KEY (CORRECT ANSWERS)

| | | | | |
|---|---|---|---|---|
| 1. | A | | 11. | C |
| 2. | B | | 12. | B |
| 3. | D | | 13. | C |
| 4. | B | | 14. | D |
| 5. | A | | 15. | B |
| 6. | B | | 16. | D |
| 7. | D | | 17. | A |
| 8. | C | | 18. | B |
| 9. | C | | | |
| 10. | A | | | |

# INTERVIEWING EXAMINATION SECTION
# TEST 1

DIRECTIONS: Each question or incomplete statement is followed by several suggested answers or completions. Select the one that BEST answers the question or completes the statement. *PRINT THE LETTER OF THE CORRECT ANSWER IN THE SPACE AT THE RIGHT.*

1. Of the following, the BEST way for an interviewer to calm a person who seems to have become emotionally upset as a result of a question asked is for the interviewer to

    A. talk to the person about other things for a short time
    B. ask that the person control himself
    C. probe for the cause of his emotional upset
    D. finish the questioning as quickly as possible

    1.____

2. You find that an applicant is hesitant about showing you some required personal material and documents. Your *initial* reaction to this situation should be to

    A. quietly insist that he give you the required materials
    B. make an exception in his case to avoid making him uncomfortable
    C. suspect that he may be trying to withhold evidence
    D. understand that he is in a stressful situation and may feel ashamed to reveal such information

    2.____

3. An applicant has just given you a response which does not seem clear.
   Of the following, the BEST course of action for you to take in order to check your understanding of the applicant's response is for you to

    A. ask the question again during a subsequent interview with this applicant
    B. repeat the applicant's answer in the applicant's own words and ask if that is what the applicant meant
    C. later in the interview, repeat the question that led to this response
    D. repeat the question that led to this response, but say it more forcefully

    3.____

4. While speaking with applicants, you may find that there are times when an applicant will be silent for a short while before answering questions.
   In order to gather the best information from the applicant, the interviewer should *generally* treat these silences by

    A. repeating the same question to make the applicant stop hesitating
    B. rephrasing the question in a way that the applicant can answer it faster
    C. directing an easier question to the applicant so that he can gain confidence in answering
    D. waiting patiently and not pressuring the applicant into quick, undeveloped answers

    4.____

5. In dealing with members of *different* ethnic and religious groups among the applicants you interview, you should give

    A. individuals the services to which they are entitled
    B. less service to those you judge to be more advantaged

    5.____

11

C. better service to groups with which you sympathize most
D. better service to groups with political "muscle"

6. You must be sure that, when interviewing an applicant, you phrase each question carefully.
Of the following, the MOST important reason for this is to insure that

   A. the applicant will phrase each of his responses carefully
   B. you use correct grammar
   C. it is clear to the applicant what information you are seeking
   D. you do not word the same question differently for different applicants

7. When given a form to complete, a client hesitates, tells you that he cannot fill out forms too well and that he is afraid he will do a poor job. He asks you to do it for him. You are quite sure, however, that he is able to do it himself.
In this case, it would be MOST advisable for you to

   A. encourage him to try filling out the application as well as he can
   B. fill out the application for him
   C. explain to him that he must learn to accept responsibility
   D. tell him that, if others can fill out an application, he can too

8. Assume that an applicant whom you are interviewing has made a statement that is obviously not true.
Of the following, the BEST course of action for you to take at this point in the interview is to

   A. ask the applicant if he is sure about his statement
   B. tell the applicant that his statement is incorrect
   C. question the applicant further to clarify his response
   D. assume that the statement is correct

9. Assume that you are conducting an *initial* interview with an applicant.
Of the following, the MOST advisable questions for you to ask at the beginning of this interview are those that

   A. can be answered in one or two sentences
   B. have nothing to do with the subject matter of the interview
   C. are most likely to reveal any hostility on the part of the applicant
   D. the applicant is most likely to be willing and able to answer

10. When interviewing a particularly nervous and upset applicant, the one of the following actions which you should take FIRST is to

    A. inform the applicant that, to be helped, he must cooperate
    B. advise the applicant that proof must be provided for statements he makes
    C. assure the applicant that every effort will be made to provide him with whatever assistance he is entitled to
    D. tell the applicant he will have no trouble so long as he is truthful

11. Assume that it is part of your job to prepare a monthly report for your unit head that eventually goes to the director. The report contains information on the number of applicants you have interviewed that have been approved and the number of applicants you have interviewed that have been turned down. Errors on such reports are *serious* because

    A. you are expected to be able to prove how many applicants you have interviewed each month
    B. accurate statistics are needed for effective management of the department
    C. they may not be discovered before the report is transmitted to the director
    D. they may result in a loss to the applicants left out of the report

12. During interviews, people give information about themselves in several ways. Which of the following *usually* gives the LEAST amount of information about the person being questioned? His

    A. spoken words
    B. tone of voice
    C. facial expression
    D. body position

13. Suppose an applicant, while being interviewed, becomes angered by your questioning and begins to use sharp, uncontrolled language.
    Which of the following is the BEST way for you to react to him?

    A. Speak in his style to show him that you are neither impressed nor upset by his speech
    B. Interrupt him and tell him that you are not required to listen to this kind of speech
    C. Lower your voice and slow the rate of your speech in an attempt to set an example that will calm him
    D. Let him continue in his way but insist that he answer your questions directly

14. You have been informed that no determination has yet been made on the eligibility of an applicant whom you have interviewed. The decision depends on further checking. His situation, however, is similar to that of many other applicants whose eligibility has been approved. The applicant, *quite worried,* calls you, and asks whether his application has been accepted.
    What would be BEST for you to do under these circumstances? Tell him

    A. his application is being checked and you will let him know the final result as soon as possible
    B. that a written request addressed to your supervisor will probably get faster action for his case
    C. not to worry since other applicants with similar backgrounds have already been accepted
    D. since there is no definite information and you are very busy, you will call him back

15. Suppose that you have been talking with an applicant. You have the feeling from the latest things the applicant has said that some of his answers to earlier questions were not totally correct. You guess that he might have been afraid or confused earlier but that your conversation has now put him in a more comfortable frame of mind.
    In order to test the reliability of information received from the earlier questions, the BEST thing for you to do *now* is to ask new questions that

A. allow the applicant to explain why he deliberately gave false information to you
B. ask for the same information, although worded differently from the original questions
C. put pressure on the applicant so that he personally wants to clear up the facts in his earlier answers
D. indicate to the applicant that you are aware of his deceptiveness

16. While providing you with required information, an applicant whom you are interviewing, informs you that she does not know certain facts.
Of the following, the MOST advisable action for you to take is to

    A. ask her to explain further
    B. advise her about research facilities
    C. express your sympathy for the situation
    D. go on to the next item of information

17. If, in an interview, you wish to determine a client's usual occupation, which one of the following questions is MOST likely to elicit the *most* useful information?

    A. Did you ever work in a factory?
    B. Do you know how to do office work?
    C. What kind of work do you do?
    D. Where are you working now?

18. Assume that you are approached by a clerk from another office who starts questioning you about one of the clients you have just interviewed. The clerk says that she is a relative of the client. According to departmental policy, all matters discussed with clients are to be kept confidential.
Of the following, the BEST course of action for you to take in this situation would be to

    A. check to see whether the clerk is really a relative before you make any further decisions
    B. explain to the clerk why you cannot divulge the information
    C. tell the clerk that you do not know the answers to her questions
    D. tell the clerk that she can get from the client any information the client wishes to give

19. Which of the following is usually the BEST technique for you, as an interviewer, to use to bring an applicant back to subject matter from which the applicant has strayed?

    A. Ask the applicant a question that is related to the subject of the interview
    B. Show the applicant that his response is unrelated to the question
    C. Discreetly reind the applicant that there is a time allotment for the interview
    D. Tell the applicant that you will be happy to discuss the extraneous matters at a future interview

20. Assume that you are interviewing a witness who is telling a story crucial to your investigation. It is important that you get all the facts being related by this witness. In order to secure this vital information, the BEST of the following techniques is to

    A. quietly interrupt the witness's story and request him to speak with deliberation so that you can record his statement
    B. guide the witness during his recital so that all important points are validated

C. confine your activities during the story to brief note-taking, and, after the information has been secured, request a full written statement
D. inform the witness that he must relate all the facts as truthfully and concisely as possible

21. The statement of any witness obtained in an interview should GENERALLY be considered

    A. as a lead requiring substantiation by additional evidence
    B. accurate if the witness appears honest and is cooperative
    C. unreliable if the witness has been involved in similar investigations
    D. as a fact admissible under the rules of evidence

22. During an important interview, an interviewer takes notes from time to time but very rarely looks at the subject being questioned.
Such action on the part of the interviewer is

    A. *unacceptable,* chiefly because during the actual interview an interviewer should pay more attention to the witness's manner of giving the information rather than to the content of his statements
    B. *acceptable,* chiefly because data should be recorded at the earliest opportunity and important data should be noted meticulously
    C. *unacceptable,* chiefly because it inhibits the person being interviewed and is not conducive to a give-and-take discussion
    D. *unacceptable,* chiefly because focusing attention on note-taking and not on the person being interviewed creates an impression of professional objectivity

23. Since he must interview persons with various personalities and attitudes, an interviewer should, *generally,* adopt a method of interviewing that

    A. is uniformly applicable to all types so that discrepancies in the accounts of individuals may be readily detected
    B. can be adjusted to the persons whom he interviews
    C. is based on the premise that most interviewees tend to be uncooperative
    D. requires the interviewer to spend as little time as possible in questioning applicants

24. One of the more difficult tasks facing an interviewer is to control the tendency of witnesses to ramble when giving information.
Of the following, the BEST technique for keeping a witness's comments pertinent is to

    A. ask questions which indicate the desired answer
    B. insist on "yes" and "no" answers to his questions
    C. construct questions that restrict the range of information which the witness can give in response
    D. ask precise questions so that the answers of the witness will necessarily be brief

25. During interviews, a certain interviewer phrases follow-up questions mentally during pauses while the subject is still answering the previous question. This practice is, *generally,*

   A. *desirable,* chiefly because it gives the impression that the interviewer is well acquainted with all the facts
   B. *undesirable,* chiefly because the interviewer cannot know whether such questions will be appropriate
   C. *desirable,* chiefly because it enables the interviewer to pose new questions without significant breaks in the discussion
   D. *undesirable,* chiefly because it subjects the person being interviewed to a barrage of questions

---

## KEY (CORRECT ANSWERS)

1. A
2. D
3. B
4. D
5. A

6. C
7. A
8. C
9. D
10. C

11. B
12. D
13. C
14. A
15. B

16. D
17. C
18. B
19. A
20. C

21. A
22. C
23. B
24. C
25. C

---

# TEST 2

DIRECTIONS: Each question or incomplete statement is followed by several suggested answers or completions. Select the one that BEST answers the question or completes the statement. *PRINT THE LETTER OF THE CORRECT ANSWER IN THE SPACE AT THE RIGHT.*

1. The one of the following which is the BEST description of a *properly* objective interviewer is one who

   A. is friendly and sensitive to the client's feelings, without becoming emotionally involved
   B. is distant and impersonal, remaining unaffected by what the client says
   C. lets personal emotions enter as far as the client's situation calls for them
   D. becomes emotionally involved with the client's situation, but without showing this involvement

   1.____

2. The one of the following which is MOST necessary for successfully intefviewing a person who belongs to a culture different from that of the interviewer is for the interviewer to

   A. have some appreciation of the other culture
   B. ignore those cultural differences which lead to bias
   C. stay away from sensitive, "touchy" issues
   D. assume the mannerisms of people in the other culture

   2.____

3. In fact-finding interviews, it is generally assumed that the smaller the lumber of interviewees, the greater the increase of reliability with the addition of others.
   The PROPER number of interviewees needed to insure the accuracy of information obtained *generally* depends upon the

   A. educational level of those interviewed
   B. number of people who have the required information
   C. directness of the questions asked
   D. variability of the information received

   3.____

4. The one of the following which is generally MOST likely to be *accurately* described in an interview by an interviewee is

   A. the presence of a large painting in the interviewer's office
   B. the number of people in the interviewer's waiting room
   C. space relations
   D. duration of time

   4.____

5. The one of the following which is *generally* the BEST course of action for an interviewer to take when interviewing a person who is reluctant to tell what he knows about a matter under investigation is to

   A. be curt and abrupt, and threaten the person with the consequences of his withholding information
   B. be firm and severe, and pressure the person into telling the needed information

   5.____

17

C. be patient and candid with the person being questioned about the investigation since doing otherwise is not ethical
D. give the person false information about the investigation so he will give the needed information without realizing its importance

6. It is often recommended that an interviewer prepare in advance a list of questions or topics to be covered in an interview.
The MAIN reason for using such a checklist is to

   A. allow investigations to be assigned to less efficient interviewers
   B. eliminate a large amount of follow-up paper work
   C. aid the interviewer in remembering to cover all important topics
   D. aid the interviewer in maintaining an objective distance from the person interviewed

6.___

7. *Usually*, the CHIEF advantage of a directive approach in an interview is that the

   A. interviewer maintains control over the course of the interview
   B. person interviewed is more likely to be put at ease
   C. person interviewed is generally left free to direct the interview
   D. interviewer will not suggest answers to the person interviewed

7.___

8. *Usually*, the CHIEF advantage of a non-directive approach in conducting an interview is that the

   A. interviewer generally conceals what he is looking for in the interview
   B. person interviewed is more likely to express his true feelings about the topic under discussion
   C. person interviewed is more likely to follow an idea introduced by the interviewer
   D. interviewer can keep the discussion limited to topics he believes to be relevant

8.___

9. The one of the following which is generally the LEAST likely to be *accurate* in a description of an event given to an interviewer is a statement about

   A. the presence of an object
   B. the number of people, when their number is small
   C. locations of people
   D. duration of time

9.___

10. Assume that you, an interviewer, are conducting a character investigation.
In an interview, the one of the following character traits of the person being interviewed which can *usually* be determined with a GOOD degree of reliability is

    A. honesty            B. dependability
    C. forcefulness       D. perseverance

10.___

11. You have been assigned the task of obtaining a family's social history.
The BEST place for you to interview members of the family while obtaining this social history would, *generally*, be in

    A. the family's home
    B. your agency's general offices
    C. the home of a friend of the family
    D. your own private office

11.___

12. If an interviewer obtains testimony from persons in interviews by means of interrogation or asking questions rather than by letting the person freely relate the testimony, what is said will, *generally,* be

    A. *greater* in range and *less* accurate
    B. *greater* in range and *more* accurate
    C. about the *same* in range and *less* accurate
    D. about the *same* in range and *more* accurate

13. Experienced interviewers have learned to phrase their questions carefully in order to obtain the desired response. Of the following, the question which would *usually* elicit the MOST accurate answer is:

    A. "How old are you?"
    B. "What is your income?"
    C. "How are you today?"
    D. "What is your date of birth?"

14. The one of the following questions which would *generally* lead to the LEAST reliable answer is:

    A. "Did you see a wallet?"
    B. "Was the German Shepherd gray?"
    C. "Didn't you see the stop sign?"
    D. "Did you see the guard on duty?"

15. Some interviewers may make a practice of observing details of the surroundings when interviewing in someone's home or office.
    Such a practice is, *generally,* considered

    A. *undesirable,* mainly because such snooping is an unwarranted, unethical invasion of privacy
    B. *undesirable,* mainly because useful information is rarely, if ever, gained this way
    C. *desirable,* mainly because useful insights into the character of the person interviewed may be gained
    D. *desirable,* mainly because it is impossible to evaluate a person adequately without such observation of his environment

# KEY (CORRECT ANSWERS)

1. A
2. A
3. D
4. A
5. C
6. C
7. A
8. B
9. D
10. C
11. A
12. A
13. D
14. B
15. C

# INTERVIEWING
# EXAMINATION SECTION
## TEST 1

DIRECTIONS: Each question or incomplete statement is followed by several suggested answers or completions. Select the one that BEST answers the question or completes the statement. *PRINT THE LETTER OF THE CORRECT ANSWER IN THE SPACE AT THE RIGHT.*

1. Of the following, the MAIN advantage to the supervisor of using the indirect (or nondirective) interview, in which he asks only guiding questions and encourages the employee to do most of the talking, is that he can
   A. obtain a mass of information about the employee in a very short period of time
   B. easily get at facts which the employee wishes to conceal
   C. get answers which are not slanted or biased in order to win his favor
   D. effectively deal with an employee's serious emotional problems

1.____

2. An interviewer under your supervision routinely closes his interview with a reassuring remark such as, "I'm sure you soon will be well," or "Everything will soon be all right."
   This practice is USUALLY considered
   A. *advisable*, chiefly because the interviewer may make the patient feel better
   B. *inadvisable*, chiefly because it may cause a patient who is seriously ill to doubt the worker's understanding of the situation
   C. *advisable*, chiefly because the patient becomes more receptive if further interviews are needed
   D. *inadvisable*, chiefly because the interviewer should usually not show that he is emotionally involved

2.____

3. An interviewer has just ushered out a client he has interviewed. As the interviewer is preparing to leave, the client mentions a fact that seems to contradict the information he has given.
   Of the following, it would be BEST for the interviewer at this time to
   A. make no response but write the fact down in his report and plan to come back another day
   B. point out to the client that he has contradicted himself and ask for an explanation
   C. ask the client to elaborate on the comment and attempt to find out further information about the fact
   D. disregard the comment since the client was probably exhausted and not thinking clearly

3.____

4. A client who is being interviewed insists on certain facts. The interviewer knows that these statements are incorrect.
   In regard to the rest of the client's statements, the interviewer is MOST justified to
   A. disregard any information the client gives which cannot be verified
   B. try to discover other misstatements by confronting the client with the discrepancy
   C. consider everything else which the client has said as the truth unless proved otherwise
   D. ask the client to prove his statements

5. Immediately after the interviewer identifies himself to a client, she says in a hysterical voice that he is not to be trusted.
   Of the following, the BEST course of action for the interviewer to follow would be to
   A. tell the woman sternly that if she does not stay calm, he will leave
   B. assure the woman that there is no cause to worry
   C. ignore the woman until she becomes quiet
   D. ask the woman to explain her problem

6. Assume that you are an interviewer and that one of your interviewees has asked you for advice on dealing with a personal problem.
   Of the following, the BEST action for you to take is to
   A. tell him about a similar problem which you know worked out well
   B. advise him not to worry
   C. explain that the problem is quite a usual one and that the situation will be brighter soon
   D. give no opinion and change the subject when practicable

7. All of the following are generally good approaches for an interviewer to use in order to improve his interviews EXCEPT
   A. developing a routine approach so that interviews can be standardized
   B. comparing his procedure with that of others engaged in similar work
   C. reviewing each interview critically, picking out one or two weak points to concentrate on improving
   D. comparing his own more successful and less successful interviews

8. Assume that a supervisor suggests at a staff meeting that digital recorders be provided for interviewers. Following are four arguments *against* the use of digital recorders that are raised by other members of the staff that might be valid:
   I. Recorded interviews provide too much unnecessary information
   II. Recorded interviews provide no record of manner or gestures
   III. Digital recorders are too cumbersome and difficult for the average supervisor to manage
   IV. Digital recorders may inhibit the interviewee

Which one of the following choices MOST accurately classifies the above into those which are generally *invalid* and those which are *not*?
- A. I and II are generally valid, but III and IV are not.
- B. IV is generally valid, but I, II, and III are not.
- C. I, II, and IV are generally valid, but III is not.
- D. I, II, III, and IV are generally valid.

9. During an interview, the PRIMARY advantage of the technique of using questions as opposed to allowing the interviewee to talk freely is that questioning
    - A. gives the interviewer greater control
    - B. provides a more complete picture
    - C. makes the interviewee more relaxed
    - D. decreases the opportunity for exaggeration

10. Assume that, in conducting an interview, an interviewer takes into consideration the age, sex, education, and background of the subject.
    This practice is GENERALLY considered
    - A. *undesirable*, mainly because an interviewer may be prejudiced by such factors
    - B. *desirable*, mainly because these are factors which might influence a person's response to certain questions
    - C. *undesirable*, mainly because these factors rarely have any bearing on the matter being investigated
    - D. *desirable*, mainly because certain categories of people answer certain questions in the same way

11. If a client should begin to tell his life story during an interview, the BEST course of action for an interviewer to take is to
    - A. interrupt immediately and insist that they return to business
    - B. listen attentively until the client finishes and then ask if they can return to the subject
    - C. pretend to have other business and come back later to see the client
    - D. interrupt politely at an appropriate point and direct the client's attention to the subject

12. An interviewer who is trying to discover the circumstances surrounding a client's accident would be MOST successful during an interview if he avoided questions which
    - A. lead the client to discuss the matter in detail
    - B. can easily be answered by either "yes" or "no"
    - C. ask for specific information
    - D. may be embarrassing or annoying to the client

13. A client being interviewed may develop an emotional reaction (positive or negative) toward the interviewer.
    The BEST attitude for the interviewer to take toward such feelings is that they are
    - A. *inevitable*; they should be accepted but kept under control
    - B. *unusual*; they should be treated impersonally

C. *obstructive*; they should be resisted at all costs
D. *abnormal*; they should be eliminated as soon as possible

14. Encouraging the client being interviewed to talk freely at first is a technique that is supported by all of the following reasons EXCEPT that it
    A. tends to counteract any preconceived ideas that the interviewer may have entertained about the client
    B. gives the interviewer a chance to learn the best method of approach to obtain additional information
    C. inhibits the client from looking to the interviewer for support and advice
    D. allows the client to reveal the answers to many questions before they are asked

15. Of the following, generally the MOST effective way for an interviewer to assure full cooperation from the client he is interviewing is to
    A. sympathize with the client's problems and assure him of concern
    B. tell a few jokes before beginning to ask questions
    C. convince the patient that the answers to the questions will help him as well as the interviewer
    D. arrange the interview when the client feels best

16. Since many elderly people are bewildered and helpless when interviewed, special consideration should be given to them.
    Of the following, the BEST way for an interviewer to *initially* approach elderly clients who express anxiety and fear is to
    A. assure them that they have nothing to worry about
    B. listen patiently and show interest in them
    C. point out the specific course of action that is best for them
    D. explain to them that many people have overcome much greater difficulties

17. Assume that, in planning an initial interview, an interviewer determines in advance what information is needed in order to fulfill the purpose of the interview.
    Of the following, this procedure usually does NOT
    A. reduce the number of additional interviews required
    B. expedite the processing of the case
    C. improve public opinion of the interviewer's agency
    D. assure the cooperation of the person interviewed

18. Sometimes an interviewer deliberately introduces his own personal interests and opinions into an interview with a client.
    In general, this practice should be considered
    A. *desirable*, primarily because the relationship between client and interviewer becomes social rather than businesslike
    B. *undesirable*, primarily because the client might complain to his supervisor
    C. *desirable*, primarily because the focus of attention is directed toward the client
    D. *undesirable*, primarily because an argument between client and interviewer could result

19. The one of the following types of interviewees who presents the LEAST difficult problem to handle is the person who
    A. answers with a great many qualifications
    B. talks at length about unrelated subjects so that the interviewer cannot ask questions
    C. has difficulty understanding the interviewer's vocabulary
    D. breaks into the middle of sentences and completes them with a meaning of his own

19.____

20. A man being interviewed is entitled to Medicaid, but he refuses to sign up for it because he says he cannot accept any form of welfare.
    Of the following, the BEST course of action for an interviewer to take FIRST is to
    A. try to discover the reason for his feeling this way
    B. tell him that he should be glad financial help is available
    C. explain that others cannot help him if he will not help himself
    D. suggest that he speak to someone who is already on Medicaid

20.____

21. Of the following, the outcome of an interview by an interviewer depend MOST heavily on the
    A. personality of the interviewee
    B. personality of the interviewer
    C. subject matter of the questions asked
    D. interaction between interviewer and interviewee

21.____

22. Some clients being interviewed by an interviewer are primarily interested in making a favorable impression.
    The interviewer should be aware of the fact that such clients are MORE likely than other clients to
    A. try to anticipate the answers the interviewer is looking for
    B. answer all questions openly and frankly
    C. try to assume the role of interviewer
    D. be anxious to get the interview over as quickly as possible

22.____

23. The type of interview which a hospital care interviewer usually conducts is *substantially different* from most interviewing situations in all of the following EXCEPT the
    A. setting                B. kinds of clients
    C. techniques employed    D. kinds of problems

23.____

24. During an interview, an interviewer uses a "leading question."
    This type of question is so-called because it *generally*
    A. starts a series of questions about one topic
    B. suggests the answer which the interviewer wants
    C. forms the basis for a following "trick" question
    D. sets, at the beginning, the tone of the interview

24.____

25. An interviewer may face various difficulties when he tries to obtain information from a client.
    Of the following, the difficulty which is EASIEST for the interviewer to overcome occurs when a client
    A. is unwilling to reveal the information
    B. misunderstands what information is needed
    C. does not have the information available to him
    D. is unable to coherently give the information requested

## KEY (CORRECT ANSWERS)

| | | | |
|---|---|---|---|
| 1. | C | 11. | D |
| 2. | B | 12. | B |
| 3. | C | 13. | A |
| 4. | C | 14. | C |
| 5. | D | 15. | C |
| 6. | D | 16. | B |
| 7. | A | 17. | D |
| 8. | C | 18. | D |
| 9. | A | 19. | C |
| 10. | B | 20. | A |

21. D
22. A
23. C
24. B
25. B

# TEST 2

DIRECTIONS: Each question or incomplete statement is followed by several suggested answers or completions. Select the one that BEST answers the question or completes the statement. *PRINT THE LETTER OF THE CORRECT ANSWER IN THE SPACE AT THE RIGHT.*

1. Of the following, the MOST appropriate manner for an interviewer to assume during an interview with a client is
   A. authoritarian   B. paternal   C. casual   D. businesslike

2. The systematic study of interviewing theory, principles, and techniques by an interviewer will USUALLY
   A. aid him to act in a depersonalized manner
   B. turn his interviewees into stereotyped affairs
   C. make the people he interviews feel manipulated
   D. give him a basis for critically examining his own practice

3. Compiling in advance a list of general questions to ask a client during an interview is a technique USUALLY considered
   A. *desirable*, chiefly because reference to the list will help keep the interview focused on the important issues
   B. *undesirable*, chiefly because use of such a list will discourage the client from speaking freely
   C. *desirable*, chiefly because the list will serve as a record of what questions were asked
   D. *undesirable*, chiefly because use of such a list will make the interview too mechanical and impersonal

4. The one of the following which is usually of GREATEST importance in winning the cooperation of a person being interviewed and while achieving the purpose of the interview is the interviewer's ability to
   A. gain the confidence of the person being interviewed
   B. stick to the subject of the interview
   C. handle a person who is obviously lying
   D. prevent the person being interviewed from withholding information

5. While interviewing clients, an interviewer should use the technique of interruption, beginning to speak when a client has temporarily paused at the end of a phrase or sentence, in order to
   A. limit the client's ability to voice his objections or complaints
   B. shorten, terminate or redirect a client's response
   C. assert authority when he feels that the client is too conceited
   D. demonstrate to the client that pauses in speech should be avoided

6. An interviewer might gain background information about a client by being aware of the person's speech during an interview.
   Which one of the following patterns of speech would offer the LEAST accurate information about a client? The

A. number of slang expressions and the level of vocabulary
B. presence and degree of an accent
C. rate of speech and the audibility level
D. presence of a physical speech defect

7. Suppose that you are interviewing a distressed client who claims that he was just laid off from his job and has no money to pay his rent.
Your FIRST action should be to
   A. ask if he has sought other employment or has other sources of income
   B. express your sympathy but explain that he must pay the rent on time
   C. inquire about the reasons he was laid off from work
   D. try to transfer him to a smaller apartment which he can afford

8. Suppose you have some background information on an applicant whom you are interviewing. During the interview, it appears that the applicant is giving you false information.
The BEST thing for you to do at that point is to
   A. pretend that you are not aware of the written facts and let him continue
   B. tell him what you already know and discuss the discrepancies with him
   C. terminate the interview and make a note that the applicant is untrustworthy
   D. tell him that, because he is making false statements, he will not be eligible for an apartment

9. A Spanish-speaking applicant may want to bring his bilingual child with him to an interview to act as an interpreter.
Which of the following would be LEAST likely to affect the value of an interview in which an applicant's child has act as interpreter?
   A. It may make it undesirable to ask certain questions.
   B. A child may do an inadequate job of interpretation.
   C. A child's answers may indicate his feelings toward his parents.
   D. The applicant may not want to reveal all information in front of his child.

10. Assume you are assigned to interview applicants.
Of the following, which is the BEST attitude for you to take in dealing with applicants?
    A. Assume they will enjoy being interviewed because they believe that you have the power of decision
    B. Expect that they have a history of anti-social behavior in the family, and probe deeply into the social development of family members
    C. Expect that they will try to control the interview, thus you should keep them on the defensive
    D. Assume that they will be polite and cooperative and attempt to secure the information you need in a business-like manner

11. If you are interviewing an applicant who is a minority group member in reference to his eligibility, it would be BEST for you to use language that is
    A. *informal*, using ethnic expressions known to the applicant
    B. *technical*, using the expressions commonly used in the agency

C. *simple*, using words and phrases which laymen understand
D. *formal* to remind the applicant that he is dealing with a government agency

12. When interviewing an applicant to determine his eligibility, it is MOST important to
    A. have a prior mental picture of the typical eligible applicant
    B. conduct the interview strictly according to a previously prepared script
    C. keep in mind the goal of the interview, which is to determine eligibility
    D. get an accurate and detailed account of the applicant's life history

13. The practice of trying to imagine yourself in the applicant's place during an interview is
    A. *good*, mainly because you will be able to evaluate his responses better
    B. *good*, mainly because it will enable you to treat him as a friend rather than as an applicant
    C. *poor*, mainly because it is important for the applicant to see you as an impartial person
    D. *poor*, mainly because it is too time-consuming to do this with each applicant

14. When dealing with clients from different ethnic backgrounds, you should be aware of certain tendencies toward prejudice.
    Which of the following statements is LEAST likely to be valid?
    A. Whites prejudiced against Blacks are more likely to be prejudiced against Hispanics than Whites not prejudiced against Blacks.
    B. The less a White is in competition with Blacks, the less likely he is to be prejudiced against them.
    C. Persons who have moved from one social group to another are likely to retain the attitudes and prejudices of their original social group.
    D. When there are few Blacks or Hispanics in a project, Whites are less likely to be prejudiced against them than when there are many.

15. Of the following, the one who is MOST likely to be a good interviewer of people seeking assistance, is one who
    A. tries to get applicants to apply to another agency instead
    B. believes that it is necessary to get as much pertinent information as possible in order to determine the applicant's real needs
    C. believes that people who seek assistance are likely to have persons with a history of irresponsible behavior in their households
    D. is convinced that there is no need for a request for assistance

## KEY (CORRECT ANSWERS)

1. D
2. D
3. A
4. A
5. B
6. C
7. A
8. B
9. C
10. D
11. C
12. C
13. A
14. C
15. B

# INTERVIEWING
# EXAMINATION SECTION
# TEST 1

DIRECTIONS: Each question or incomplete statement is followed by several suggested answers or completions. Select the one that BEST answers the question or completes the statement. *PRINT THE LETTER OF THE CORRECT ANSWER IN THE SPACE AT THE RIGHT.*

1. You are conducting an interview with a client who has been having some difficulties with one of her fellow-workers. The client walks on crutches. You tell the client that she probably finds it difficult to get along with her fellow-workers because of this handicap.
   To make such a statement would, *generally*, be

   A. *proper;* people are often prejudiced against persons with physical deformities
   B. *proper;* statements such as this indicate to the client that you are sympathetic toward her
   C. *improper;* this approach would not help the client solve her problem
   D. *improper;* you should have discussed this handicap in relation to the client's continued ability to continue in her job

2. The information which the interviewer plans to secure from an individual with whom he talks is determined MAINLY by the

   A. purpose of the interview and the functions of the agency
   B. state assistance laws and the desires of the individual
   C. privacy they have while talking and the willingness of the individual to give information
   D. emotional feelings of the individual seeking help and the interviewer's reactions to these feelings

3. *Generally,* the MOST effective of the following ways of dealing with a person being interviewed who frequently digresses from the subject under discussion or starts to ramble, is for the interviewer to

   A. tell the person that he, the interviewer, will have to terminate the interview unless the former sticks to the point
   B. increase the tempo of the interview
   C. demonstrate that he is a good listener and allow the person to continue in his own way
   D. inject questions which relate to the purpose of the interview

4. "Being a good listener" is an interviewing technique which, if applied properly, is *desirable* MOSTLY because it

   A. catches the client more easily in misrepresentations and lies
   B. conserves the energies of the interviewer
   C. encourages the client to talk about his personal affairs without restraint
   D. encourages the giving of information which is generally more reliable and complete

5. When questioning applicants for eligibility, it would be BEST to ask questions that are

A. *direct,* so that the applicant will realize that the interviewer knows what he is doing
B. *direct,* so that the information received will be as pertinent as possible
C. *indirect,* so that the applicant will not realize the purpose of the interview
D. *indirect,* so that you can trap the applicant into making admissions that he would not otherwise make

6. The CHIEF reason for conducting an interview with a new applicant in complete privacy is that the

   A. interviewer will be better able to record the facts without any other worker reading his case notes
   B. applicant will be impressed by the business-like atmosphere of the agency
   C. interviewer will be able to devote more time to questioning the applicant without interruption
   D. applicant will be more likely to speak frankly

7. When conducting an interview with a client who is upset because of an increase in rent, it would be BEST for the interviewer to

   A. agree with the client that the agency was wrong in raising his rent, as a basis for further discussion
   B. tell the client that unless he calms down the interview will be ended
   C. prevent the client from becoming emotional
   D. tell the client the reasons for the increase

8. At an interview to determine whether an applicant is eligible, the applicant gives information different from that which he submitted on his application.
   The MOST advisable action to take is to

   A. cross out the old information, enter the new information, and initial the entry
   B. re-enter the old information on the application form and initial the entry
   C. give the applicant another application form, have him fill it out correctly, and resume the interview
   D. give the applicant another application form to fill out, and set a later date for another interview

9. After you have secured, in an interview, all the necessary information from an applicant, he shows no intention of leaving, but starts to tell you a long personal story.
   Of the following, the MOST advisable action for you to take is to

   A. explain to the applicant why personal stories are out of place in a business office
   B. listen carefully to the story for whatever relevant information it may contain
   C. interrupt him tactfully, thank him for the information he has already given, and terminate the interview
   D. inform your supervisor that the time required for this interview will prevent you from completing the interviews scheduled for the day

10. In interviewing, the practice of anticipating an applicant's answers to questions is, *generally,*

    A. *desirable* because it is effective and economical when it is necessary to interview large numbers of applicants
    B. *desirable* because many applicants have language difficulties

C. *undesirable* because it is the inalienable right of every person to answer as he sees fit
D. *undesirable* because applicants may tend to agree with the answer proposed by the interviewer even when the answer is not entirely correct

11. A follow-up interview was arranged for an applicant in order that he might furnish certain requested evidence. At this follow-up interview, the applicant still fails to furnish the necessary evidence.
    It would be MOST advisable for you to

    A. advise the applicant that he is now considered ineligible
    B. ask the applicant how soon he can get the necessary evidence and set a date for another interview
    C. question the applicant carefully and thoroughly to determine if he has misrepresented or falsified any information
    D. set a date for another interview and tell the applicant to get the necessary evidence by that time

12. When an initial interview is being conducted, one way of starting is to explain the purpose of the interview to the applicant.
    The practice of starting the interview with such an explanation is, *generally,*

    A. *desirable* because the applicant can then understand why the interview is necessary and what will be accomplished by it
    B. *desirable* because it creates the rapport which is necessary to successful interviewing
    C. *undesirable* because time will be saved by starting off directly with the questions which must be asked
    D. *undesirable* because the interviewer should have the choice of starting an interview in any manner he prefers

13. Empathy can be defined as the ability of one individual to respond sensitively and imaginatively to another's feelings.
    For an interviewer to be empathic during an interview is *usually*

    A. *undesirable,* mainly because an interviewer should never be influenced by the feelings of the one being interviewed
    B. *desirable,* mainly because an interview will not be productive unless the interviewer takes the side of the person interviewed
    C. *undesirable,* mainly because empathy usually leads an interviewer to be biased in favor of the person being interviewed
    D. *desirable,* mainly because this ability allows the interviewer to direct his questions more effectively to the person interviewed

14. Assume that you must interview several people who know each other.
    To gather them all in one group and question them TOGETHER, is, *generally,*

    A. *good practice,* since any inaccurate information offered by one person would be corrected by others in the group
    B. *poor practice,* since people in a group rarely pay adequate attention to questions
    C. *good practice,* since the interviewer will save much time and effort in this way
    D. *poor practice,* since the presence of several people can inhibit an individual from speaking

15. An effective interviewer should know that the one of the following reasons which LEAST describes why there is a wide range of individual behavior in human relations is that

    A. socio-economic status influences human behavior
    B. physical characteristics do not influence human behavior
    C. education influences human behavior
    D. childhood experience influences human behavior

16. An interviewer encounters an uncooperative interviewee. Of the following, the FIRST thing the interviewer should do in such a situation is to

    A. try various appeals to win the interviewee over to a cooperative attitude
    B. try to ascertain the reason for non-cooperation
    C. promise the interviewee that all data will be kept confidential
    D. alter his interviewing technique with the uncooperative interviewee

17. You discover that an interviewee who was requested to bring with him specific documents for his initial employment interview has forgotten the documents.
    Of the following, the BEST course of action to take is to

    A. give the person a reasonable amount of time to furnish the documents
    B. tell the person you will let him know how much additional time he has
    C. mark the person disqualified for employment; he has failed to provide reasonably requested data on time
    D. mark the person provisionally qualified for employment; upon receipt of the documents he will be permanently qualified

18. In checking interviewees' work experience, you realize that the person whom you are to interview is only marginally fluent in English and has, therefore, requested permission to bring a translator with him.
    Of the following, the BEST course of action is to inform the interviewee that

    A. outside translators may not be used
    B. only city translators may be used
    C. state law requires fluency in English of all civil servants
    D. he may be assisted in the interview by his translator

19. Assume that, during the course of an interview, you are verbally attacked by the person being interviewed.
    Of the following, it would be MOST advisable to

    A. answer back in a matter-of-fact manner
    B. ask the person to apologize and discontinue the interview
    C. ignore the attack but adjourn the interview to another day
    D. use restraint and continue the interview

20. Assume that you find that the person you are interviewing has difficulty finishing his sentences and seems to be groping for words.
    In such a case, the BEST approach for you to take is to

    A. say what you think the person has in mind
    B. proceed patiently without calling attention to the problem
    C. ask the person why he finds it difficult to finish his sentences
    D. interrupt the interview until the person feels more relaxed

21. The one of the following which BEST describes the effect of the *sympathetic approach* in interviewing on the interviewee is that it will     21.____

    A. have no discernible effect on the interviewee
    B. calm the interviewee
    C. lead the interviewee to underemphasize his problems
    D. mislead the interviewee

22. The one of the following characteristics which is a PRIMARY requisite for a successful interview is     22.____

    A. total *curiosity*            B. total *sympathy*
    C. complete *attention*         D. complete *dedication*

23. Assume that you have been assigned to conduct a follow-up interview with a primary witness.     23.____
    The one of the following which is MOST important in arranging such an interview is to

    A. keep the witness cooperative
    B. conduct the matter in secret
    C. allow the witness to determine where and when the interview takes place
    D. conduct the interview as soon as possible to insure a strong case

24. By examining a candidate's employment record, an interviewer can determine many things about the candidate. Of the following, the one which is LEAST apparent from an employment record is the candidate's     24.____

    A. character
    B. willingness to work
    C. capacity to get along with co-workers
    D. potential for advancing in civil service

25. Assume that you are conducting an interview in which the person being interviewed is using the interview as a forum for venting his anti-civil service feelings.     25.____
    Of the following, the FIRST thing that you should do is to

    A. agree with the person; perhaps that will shorten the outburst
    B. respectfully disagree with the person; the decorum of the interview has already been disrupted
    C. courteously and objectively direct the interview to the relevant issue
    D. reschedule the interview to another mutually agreeable time

## KEY (CORRECT ANSWERS)

| | | | |
|---|---|---|---|
| 1. | C | 11. | B |
| 2. | A | 12. | A |
| 3. | D | 13. | D |
| 4. | D | 14. | D |
| 5. | B | 15. | B |
| 6. | D | 16. | B |
| 7. | D | 17. | A |
| 8. | A | 18. | D |
| 9. | C | 19. | D |
| 10. | D | 20. | B |

21. C
22. C
23. A
24. D
25. C

# TEST 2

DIRECTIONS: Each question or incomplete statement is followed by several suggested answers or completions. Select the one that BEST answers the question or completes the statement. *PRINT THE LETTER OF THE CORRECT ANSWER IN THE SPACE AT THE RIGHT.*

1. The pattern of an interview is LARGELY set by the     1.____

    A. person being interviewed
    B. person conducting the interview
    C. nature of the interview
    D. policy of the agency employing the interviewer

2. Assume that a person being interviewed, who had been talking freely, suddenly tries to change the subject.     2.____
    To a trained interviewer, this behavior would mean that the person *probably*

    A. knew very little about the subject
    B. realized that he was telling too much
    C. decided that his privacy was being violated
    D. realized that he was becoming confused

3. Assume that you receive a telephone call from an unknown individual requesting information about a person you are currently interviewing.     3.____
    In such a situation, the BEST course of action for you to take is to

    A. give him the information over the telephone
    B. tell him to write to your department for the information
    C. send him the information, retaining a copy for your files
    D. tell him to call back, giving you additional time to check into the matter

4. In an interview, assuming that the interviewer was using a *non-directive approach* in this interview, of the following, the interviewer's most effective response would be:     4.____

    A. "You know, you are building a bad record of tardiness."
    B. "Can you tell me more about this situation?"
    C. "What kind of person is your superior?"
    D. "Do you think you are acting fairly towards the agency by being late so often?"

5. In an interview, assuming that the interviewer was using a *directed approach* in this interview, of the following, the interviewer's response should be:     5.____

    A. "That doesn't seem like much of an excuse to me."
    B. "What do you mean by saying that you've lost interest?"
    C. "What problems are there with the supervision you are getting?"
    D. "How do you think your tardiness looks in your personnel record?"

Questions 6-8.

DIRECTIONS: Answer Questions 6 through 8 only on the basis of information given in the passage below.

A personnel interviewer, selecting job applicants, may find that he reacts badly to some people even on first contact. This reaction cannot usually be explained by things that the interviewee has done or said. Most of us have had the experience of liking or disliking, of feeling comfortable or uncomfortable with people on first acquaintance, long before we have had a chance to make a conscious, rational decision about them. Often, too, our liking or disliking is transmitted to the other person by subtle processes such as gestures, posture, voice intonations, or choice of words. The point to be kept in mind in this: the relations between people are complex and occur at several levels, from the conscious to the unconscious. This is true whether the relationship is brief or long, formal or informal.

Some of the major dynamics of personality which operate on the unconscious level are projection, sublimation, rationalization, and repression. Encountering these for the first time, one is apt to think of them as representing pathological states. In the extreme, they undoubtedly are, but they exist so universally that we must consider them also to be parts of normal personality.

Without necessarily subscribing to any of the numerous theories of personality, it is possible to describe personality in terms of certain important aspects or elements. We are all aware of ourselves as thinking organisms.

This aspect of personality, the conscious part, is important for understanding human behavior, but it is not enough. Many find it hard to accept the notion that each person also has an unconscious. The existence of the unconscious is no longer a matter of debate. It is not possible to estimate at all precisely what proportion of our total psychological life is conscious, what proportion unconscious. Everyone who has studied the problem, however, agrees that consciousness is the smaller part of personality. Most of what we are and do is a result of unconscious processes. To ignore this is to risk mistakes.

6. The passage above suggests that an interviewer can be MOST effective if he 6.____

   A. learns how to determine other peoples' unconscious motivations
   B. learns how to repress his own unconsciously motivated mannerisms and behavior
   C. can keep others from feeling that he either likes or dislikes them
   D. gains an understanding of how the unconscious operates in himself and in others

7. It may be inferred from the passage above that the "subtle processes, such as gestures, posture, voice intonation, or choice of words," referred to in the first paragraph, are, *usually*, 7.____

   A. in the complete control of an expert interviewer
   B. the determining factors in the friendships a person establishes
   C. controlled by a person's unconscious
   D. not capable of being consciously controlled

8. The passage above implies that various different personality theories are, *usually*, 8.____

   A. so numerous and different as to be valueless to an interviewer
   B. in basic agreement about the importance of the unconscious
   C. understood by the interviewer who strives to be effective
   D. in agreement that personality factors such as projection and repression are pathological

Questions 9-10.

DIRECTIONS: Answer Questions 9 and 10 ONLY on the basis of information given in the passage below.

Since we generally assure informants that what they say is confidential, we are not free to tell one informant what the other has told us. Even if the informant says, "I don't care who knows it; tell anybody you want to," we find it wise to treat the interview as confidential. An interviewer who relates to some informants what other informants have told him is likely to stir up anxiety and suspicion. Of course, the interviewer may be able to tell an informant what he has heard without revealing the source of his information. This may be perfectly appropriate where a story has wide currency so that an informant cannot infer the source of the information. But if an event is not widely known, the mere mention of it may reveal to one informant what another informant has said about the situation. How can the data be cross-checked in these circumstances?

9. The passage above implies that the anxiety and suspicion an interviewer may arouse by telling what has been learned in other interviews is due to the

   A. lack of trust the person interviewed may have in the interviewer's honesty
   B. troublesome nature of the material which the interviewer has learned in other interviews
   C. fact that the person interviewed may not believe that permission was given to repeat the information
   D. fear of the person interviewed that what he is telling the interviewer will be repeated

10. The paragraph above is *most likely* part of a longer passage dealing with

    A. ways to verify data gathered in interviews
    B. the various anxieties a person being interviewed may feel
    C. the notion that people sometimes say things they do not mean
    D. ways an interviewer can avoid seeming suspicious

Questions 11-12.

DIRECTIONS: Answer Questions 11 and 12 ONLY on the basis of information given below.

The ability to interview rests not only on any single trait, but on a vast complex of them. Habits, skills, techniques, and attitudes are all involved. Competence in interviewing is acquired only after careful and diligent study, prolonged practice (preferably under supervision), and a good bit of trial and error; for interviewing is not an exact science, it is an art. Like many other arts, however, it can and must draw on science in several of its aspects.

There is always a place for individual initiative, for imaginative innovations, and for new combinations of old approaches. The skilled interviewer cannot be bound by a set of rules. Likewise, there is not a set of rules which can guarantee to the novice that his interviewing will be successful. There are, however, some accepted, general guide-posts which may help the beginner to avoid mistakes, learn how to conserve his efforts, and establish effective working relationships with interviewees; to accomplish, in short, what he set out to do.

11. According to the passage above, rules and standard techniques for interviewing are

A. helpful for the beginner, but useless for the experienced, innovative interviewer
B. destructive of the innovation and initiative needed for a good interviewer
C. useful for even the experienced interviewer, who may, however, sometimes go beyond them
D. the means by which nearly anybody can become an effective interviewer

12. According to the passage above, the one of the following which is a prerequisite to competent interviewing is    12.____

    A. avoiding mistakes
    B. study and practice
    C. imaginative innovation
    D. natural aptitude

Questions 13-16.

DIRECTIONS: Answer Questions 13 through 16 SOLELY on the basis of information given in the following paragraph.

The question of what material is relevant is not as simple as it might seem. Frequently material which seems irrelevant to the inexperienced has, because of the common tendency to disguise and distort and misplace one's feelings, considerable significance. It may be necessary to let the client "ramble on" for a while in order to clear the decks, as it were, so that he may get down to things that really are on his mind. On the other hand, with an already disturbed person, it may be important for the interviewer to know when to discourage further elaboration of upsetting material. This is especially the case where the worker would be unable to do anything about it. An inexperienced interviewer might, for instance, be intrigued with the bizarre elaboration of material that the psychotic produces, but further elaboration of this might encourage the client in his instability. A too random discussion may indicate that the interviewee is not certain in what areas the interviewer is prepared to help him, and he may be seeking some direction. Or again, satisfying though it may be for the interviewer to have the interviewee tell him intimate details, such revelations sometimes need to be checked or encouraged only in small doses. An interviewee who has "talked too much" often reveals subsequent anxiety. This is illustrated by the fact that? frequently after a "confessional" interview ,the interviewee surprises the interviewer by being withdrawn, inarticulate, or hostile, or by breaking the next appointment.

13. Sometimes a client may reveal certain personal information to an interviewer and subsequently, may feel anxious about this revelation.    13.____
    If, during an interview, a client begins to discuss very personal matters, it would be BEST to

    A. tell the client, in no uncertain terms, that you're not interested in personal details
    B. ignore the client at this point
    C. encourage the client to elaborate further on the details
    D. inform the client that the information seems to be very personal

14. Clients with severe psychological disturbances pose an especially difficult problem for the inexperienced interviewer.
The difficulty lies in the possibility of the client's

    A. becoming physically violent and harming the interviewer
    B. "rambling on" for a while
    C. revealing irrelevant details which may be followed by cancelled appointments
    D. reverting to an unstable state as a result of interview material

14.____

15. An interviewer should be constantly alert to the possibility of obtaining clues from the client as to problem areas.
According to the above passage, a client who discusses topics at random may be

    A. unsure of what problems the interviewer can provide help
    B. reluctant to discuss intimate details
    C. trying to impress the interviewer with his knowledge
    D. deciding what relevant material to elaborate on

15.____

16. The evaluation of a client's responses may reveal substantial information that may aid the interviewer in assessing the problem areas that are of concern to the client. Responses that seemed irrelevant at the time of the interview may be of significance because

    A. considerable significance is attached to all irrelevant material
    B. emotional feelings are frequently masked
    C. an initial "rambling on" is often a prelude to what -is actually bothering the client
    D. disturbed clients often reveal subsequent anxiety

16.____

Questions 17-19.

DIRECTIONS: Answer Questions 17 through 19 SOLELY on the basis of the following paragraph.

The physical setting of the interview may determine its entire potentiality. Some degree of privacy and a comfortable relaxed atmosphere are important. The interviewee is not encouraged to give much more than his name and address if the interviewer seems busy with other things, if people are rushing about, if there are distracting noises. He has a right to feel that, whether the interview lasts five minutes or an hour, he has, for that time, the undivided attention of the interviewer. Interruptions, telephone calls, and so on, should be reduced to a minimum. If the interviewee has waited in a crowded room for what seems to him an interminably long period, he is naturally in no mood to sit down and discuss what is on his mind. Indeed, by that time the primary thing on his mind may be his irritation at being kept waiting, and he frequently feels it would be impolite to express this. If a wait or interruptions have been unavoidable, it is always helpful to give the client some recognition that these are disturbing and that he can naturally understand that they make it more difficult for him to proceed. At the same time if he protests that they have not troubled him, the interviewer can best accept his statements at their face value, as further insistence that they must have been disturbing may be interpreted by him as accusing, and he may conclude that the interviewer has been personally hurt by his irritation.

17. Distraction during an interview may tend to limit the client's responses. In a case where an interruption has occurred, it would be BEST for the interviewer to

    A. terminate this interview and have it rescheduled for another time period
    B. ignore the interruption since it is not continuous
    C. express his understanding that the distraction can cause the client to feel disturbed
    D. accept the client's protests that he has been troubled by the interruption

18. To maximize the rapport that can be established with the client, an appropriate physical setting is necessary. At the very least, some privacy would be necessary.
    *In addition,* the interviewer should

    A. always appear to be busy in order to impress the client
    B. focus his attention only on the client
    C. accept all the client's statements as being valid
    D. stress the importance of the interview to the client

19. Clients who have been waiting quite some time for their interview may, justifiably, become upset. However, a client *may initially* attempt to mask these feelings because he may

    A. personally hurt the interviewer
    B. want to be civil
    C. feel that the wait was unavoidable
    D. fear the consequences of his statement

20. You have been assigned to interview W, a witness, concerning a minor automobile accident. Although you have made no breach of the basic rules of contact and approach, you, nevertheless, recognize that you and W have a personality clash and that a natural animosity has resulted.
    Of the following, you MOST appropriately should

    A. discuss the personality problem with W and attempt to resolve the difference
    B. stop the interview on some pretext and leave in a calm and pleasant manner, allowing an associate to continue the interview
    C. ignore the personality problem and continue as though nothing had happened
    D. change the subject matter being discussed since the facts sought may be the source of the animosity

21. Assume that you desire to interview W, a reluctant witness to an event that took place several weeks previously. Assume further that the interview can take place at a location to be designated by the interviewer.
    Of the following, the place of interview should *preferably* be the

    A. office of the interviewer
    B. home of W
    C. office of W
    D. scene where the event took place

22. Assume that you are interviewing W, a witness. During the interview it becomes apparent that W's statements are inaccurate and at variance with the facts previously established. In these circumstances, it would be BEST for you to

    A. tell W that his statements are inaccurate and point out how they conflict with previously established facts

B. reword your questions and ask additional questions about the facts being discussed
C. warn W that he may be required to testify under oath at a later date
D. ignore W's statements if you have other information that support the facts

23. Assume that W, a witness being interviewed by you, shows a tendency to ramble. His answers to your questions are lengthy and not responsive.
In this situation, the BEST action for you to take is to

   A. permit W to continue because at some point he will tell you the information sought
   B. tell W that he is rambling and unresponsive and that more will be accomplished if he is brief and to the point
   C. control the interview so that complete and accurate information is obtained
   D. patiently listen to W since rambling is W's style and it cannot be changed

24. Assume that you are interviewing a client. Of the following, the BEST procedure for you to follow in regard to the use of your notebook is to

   A. take out your notebook at the start of the interview and immediately begin taking notes
   B. memorize the important facts related during the interview and enter them after the interview has been completed
   C. advise the client that all his answers are being taken down to insure that he will tell the truth
   D. establish rapport with the client and ask permission to jot down various data in your notebook

25. In order to conduct an effective interview, an interviewer's attention must continuously be directed in two ways, toward himself as well as toward the interviewee. Of the following, the PRIMARY danger in this division of attention is that the

   A. interviewer's behavior may become less natural and thus alienate the interviewee
   B. interviewee's span of attention will be shortened
   C. interviewer's response may be interpreted by the interviewee as being antagonistic
   D. interviewee's more or less concealed prejudices will come to the surface

8 (#2)

# KEY (CORRECT ANSWERS)

| | | | |
|---|---|---|---|
| 1. | B | 11. | C |
| 2. | B | 12. | B |
| 3. | B | 13. | D |
| 4. | B | 14. | D |
| 5. | C | 15. | A |
| 6. | D | 16. | B |
| 7. | C | 17. | C |
| 8. | B | 18. | B |
| 9. | D | 19. | B |
| 10. | A | 20. | B |

21. A
22. B
23. C
24. D
25. A

———

# EXAMINATION SECTION
# TEST 1

DIRECTIONS: Each question or incomplete statement is followed by several suggested answers or completions. Select the one that *BEST* answers the question or completes the statement. *PRINT THE LETTER OF THE CORRECT ANSWER IN THE SPACE AT THE RIGHT.*

1. When a counselor is planning a future interview with a client, of the following, the MOST important consideration is the    1.____

    A. recommendations he will make to the client
    B. place where the client will be interviewed
    C. purpose for which the client will be interviewed
    D. personality of the client

2. For a counselor to make a practice of reviewing the client's case record, if available, prior to the interview, is, usually,    2.____

    A. *inadvisable,* because knowledge of the client's past record will tend to influence the counselor's judgment
    B. *advisable,* because knowledge of the client's background will help the counselor to identify discrepancies in the client's responses
    C. *inadvisable,* because such review is time-consuming and of questionable value
    D. *advisable,* because knowledge of the client's background will help the counselor to understand the client's situation

3. Assume that a counselor makes a practice of constantly reassuring clients with serious and complex problems by making such statements as: "I'm sure you'll soon be well;" "I know you'll get a job soon;" or "Everything will be all right."
Of the following, the MOST likely result of such a practice is to    3.____

    A. encourage the client and make him feel that the counselor understands what the client is going through
    B. make the client doubtful about the counselor's understanding of his difficulties and the counselor's ability to help
    C. confuse the client and cause him to hesitate to take any action on his own initiative
    D. help the client to be more realistic about his situation and the probability that it will improve

4. In order to get the maximum amount of information from a client during an interview, of the following, it is MOST important for the counselor to communicate to the client the feeling that the counselor is    4.____

    A. interested in the client
    B. a figure of authority
    C. efficient in his work habits
    D. sympathetic to the client's lifestyle

5. Of the following, the counselor who takes extremely detailed notes during an interview with a client is *most likely* to    5.____

    A. encourage the client to talk freely

B. distract and antagonize the client
C. help the client feel at ease
D. understand the client's feelings

6. As a counselor, you find that many of the clients you interview are verbally abusive and unusually hostile to you.
   Of the following, the MOST appropriate action for you to take *first* is to

   A. review your interviewing techniques and consider whether you may be provoking these clients
   B. act in a more authoritative manner when interviewing troublesome clients
   C. tell these clients that you will not process their applications unless their troublesome behavior ceases
   D. disregard the clients' troublesome behavior during the interview

7. During an interview, you did not completely understand several of your client's responses. In each instance, you rephrased the client's statement and asked the client if that was what he meant.
   For you to use such a technique during interviews would be considered

   A. *inappropriate;* you may have distorted the client's meaning by rephrasing his statements
   B. *inappropriate;* you should have asked the same questioE until you received a comprehensible response
   C. *appropriate;* the client will have a chance to correct you if you have misinterpreted his responses
   D. *appropriate;* a counselor should rephrase clients' responses for the records

8. A counselor is interviewing a client who has just had a severe emotional shock because of an assault on her by a mugger.
   Of the following, the approach which would generally be MOST helpful to the client is for the counselor to

   A. comfort the client and encourage her to talk about the assault
   B. sympathize with the client but refuse to discuss the assault with her
   C. tell the client to control her emotions and think positively about the future
   D. proceed with the interview in an impersonal and unemotional manner

9. A counselor finds that her questions are misinterpreted by many of the clients she interviews.
   Of the following, the MOST likely reason for this problem is that the

   A. client is not listening attentively
   B. client wants to avoid the subject being discussed
   C. counselor has failed to express her meaning clearly
   D. counselor has failed to put the client at ease

10. For a counselor to look directly at the client and observe him during the interview is generally

    A. *inadvisable;* this will make the client nervous and uncomfortable
    B. *advisable;* the client will be more likely to refrain from lying
    C. *inadvisable;* the counselor will not be able to take notes for the case record
    D. *advisable;* this will encourage conversation and accelerate the progress of the interview

11. You are interviewing a client who is applying for social services for the first time. In order to encourage this client to freely give you the information needed for you to establish his eligibility, of the following, the BEST way to start the interview is by

    A. asking questions the client can easily answer
    B. conveying the impression that his responses to your questions will be checked
    C. asking two or three similar but important questions
    D. assuring the client that your sole responsibility is "getting the facts"

11.____

12. Counselors are encouraged to record significant information obtained from clients and services provided for clients. Of the following, the MOST important reason for this practice is that these case records will

    A. help to reduce the need for regular supervisory conferences
    B. indicate to counselors which clients are taking up the most time
    C. provide information which will help the agency to improve its services to clients
    D. make it easier to verify the complaints of clients

12.____

13. As a counselor you find that interviews can be completed in a shorter period of time if you ask questions which limit the client to a certain answer.
    For you to use such a technique would be considered

    A. *inappropriate,* because this type of question usually requires advance preparation
    B. *inappropriate,* because this type of question may inhibit the client from saying what he really means
    C. *appropriate,* because you know the areas into which the questions should be directed
    D. *appropriate,* because this type of question usually helps clients to express themselves clearly

13.____

14. Assume that, while you are interviewing an individual to obtain information, the individual pauses in the middle of an answer.
    The BEST of the following actions for you to take at this time is to

    A. correct any inaccuracies in what he has said
    B. remain silent until he continues
    C. explain your position on the matter being discussed
    D. explain that time is short and that he must complete his story quickly

14.____

15. You have been assigned to interview the mother of a five-year-old son in her home to get information useful in locating the child's absent father. During the interview, you notice many serious bruises on the child's arms and legs, which the mother explains are due to the child's clumsiness. Of the following, your BEST course of action is to

    A. accept the mother's explanation and concentrate on getting information which will help you to locate the father
    B. advise the mother to have the child examined for a medical condition that may be causing his clumsiness
    C. make a surprise visit to the mother later, to see if someone is beating the child
    D. complete your interview with the mother and report the case to your supervisor for investigation of possible child abuse

15.____

16. During an interview, the former landlord of an absent father offers to help you to locate the father if you will give the landlord confidential information you have on the financial situation of the father.
    Of the following, you should

    A. immediately end the interview with the landlord
    B. urge the landlord to help you but explain that you are not permitted to give him confidential information
    C. freely give the landlord the confidential information he requests about the father
    D. give the landlord the information only if he promises to keep it confidential

17. You feel that your client, a released mental patient, is not adjusting well to living on his own in an apartment. To gather more information, you interview privately his next-door neighbor, who claims that the client is creating a "disturbance" and speaks of the client in an angry and insulting manner.
    Of the following, the BEST action for you to take in this situation is to

    A. listen patiently to the neighbor to try to get the facts about your client's behavior
    B. inform the neighbor that he has no right to speak insultingly about a mentally ill person
    C. make an appointment to interview the neighbor some other time when he isn't so upset
    D. tell the neighbor that you were not aware of the client's behavior and that you will have the client moved

18. As a counselor, you are interviewing a client to determine his eligibility for a work program. Suddenly the client begins to shout that he is in no condition to work and that you are persecuting him for no reason.
    Of the following, your BEST response to this client is to

    A. advise the client to stop shouting or you will call for the security guard
    B. wait until the client calms down, then order him to come back for another interview
    C. insist that you are not persecuting the client and that he must complete the interview
    D. wait until the client calms down, say that you understand how he feels, and try to continue the interview

19. You are interviewing a mother whose 17-year-old son has recently been returned home from a mental institution. Although she is willing to care for her son at home, she is frightened by his strange and sometimes violent behavior and does not know the best arrangement to make for his care.
    Of the following, your MOST appropriate response to this mother's problem is to

    A. describe the supportive services and alternatives to home care which are available
    B. help her to accept her son's strange and violent behavior
    C. tell her that she will not be permitted to care for her son at home if she is frightened by his behavior
    D. convince her that she is not responsible for her son's mental condition

20. Assume that you are interviewing an elderly man who comes to the center several times a month to discuss topics with you which are not related to social services. You realize that the man is lonely and enjoys these conversations.
    Of the following, it would be MOST appropriate to

    A. politely discourage the man from coming in to pass the time with you
    B. avoid speaking to this man the next time he comes into the center
    C. explore with the client his feelings about joining a senior citizens' center
    D. continue to hold these conversations with the man

21. A client you are interviewing tends to ramble on after each response that he gives, so that many clients are kept waiting.
    In this situation, of the following, it would be MOST advisable to

    A. try to direct the interview, in order to obtain the necessary information
    B. reduce the number of questions asked so that you can shorten the interview
    C. arrange a second interview for the client so that you can give him more time
    D. tell the client that he is wasting everybody's time

22. A non-minority counselor is about to interview a minority client on public assistance for job placement when the client says: "What does your kind know about my problems? You've never had to survive out on these streets."
    Of the following, the counselor's MOST appropriate response in this situation is to

    A. postpone the interview until a minority counselor is available to interview the client
    B. tell the client that he must cooperate with the counselor if he wants to continue receiving public assistance
    C. explain to the client the function of the counselor in this unit and the services he provides
    D. assure the client that you do not have to be a member of a minority group to understand the effects of poverty

23. When you are interviewing someone to obtain information, the BEST of the following reasons for you to repeat certain of his exact words is to

    A. *assure* him that appropriate action will be taken
    B. *encourage* him to elaborate on a point he has made
    C. *assure* him that you agree with his point of view
    D. *encourage* him to switch to another topic of discussion

24. You are interviewing a young client who seriously under-estimates the amount of education and training he will require for a certain occupation.
    For you to tell the client that you think he is mistaken would generally be considered

    A. *inadvisable*, because counselors should not express their opinions to clients
    B. *inadvisable*, because clients have the right to self-determination
    C. *advisable*, because clients should generally be alerted to their misconceptions
    D. *advisable*, because counselors should convince clients to adopt a proper life style

25. Of the following, the MOST appropriate manner for a counselor to assume during an interview with a patient is

    A. authoritarian
    B. paternal
    C. casual
    D. businesslike

25. _____

---

# KEY (CORRECT ANSWERS)

| | | | |
|---|---|---|---|
| 1. | C | 11. | A |
| 2. | D | 12. | C |
| 3. | B | 13. | B |
| 4. | A | 14. | B |
| 5. | B | 15. | D |
| 6. | A | 16. | B |
| 7. | C | 17. | A |
| 8. | A | 18. | D |
| 9. | C | 19. | A |
| 10. | D | 20. | C |

| | |
|---|---|
| 21. | A |
| 22. | C |
| 23. | B |
| 24. | C |
| 25. | D |

# TEST 2

DIRECTIONS: Each question or incomplete statement is followed by several suggested answers or completions. Select the one that BEST answers the question or completes the statement. *PRINT THE LETTER OF THE CORRECT ANSWER IN THE SPACE AT THE RIGHT.*

1. You are interviewing a legally responsible absent father who refuses to make child support payments because he claims the mother physically abuses the child.
   Of the following, the BEST way for you to handle this situation is to tell the father that you

   A. will report his complaint about the mother, but he is still responsible for making child support payments
   B. suspect that he is complaining about the mother in order to avoid his own responsibility for making child support payments
   C. are concerned with his responsibility to make child support payments, not with the mother's abuse of the child
   D. can not determine his responsibility for making child support payments until his complaint about the mother is investigated

   1.____

2. You are interviewing an elderly woman who lives alone to determine her eligibility for homemaker service at public expense. Though obviously frail and in need of this service, the woman is not completely cooperative, and during the interview, is often silent for a considerable period of time.
   Of the following, the BEST way for you to deal with these periods of silence is to

   A. realize that she may be embarrassed to have to apply for homemaker service at public expense, and emphasize her right to this service
   B. postpone the interview and make an appointment with her for a later date, when she may be better able to cooperate
   C. explain to the woman that you have many clients to interview and need her cooperation to complete the interview quickly
   D. recognize that she is probably hiding something and begin to ask questions to draw her out

   2.____

3. During a conference with an adolescent boy at a juvenile detention center, you find out for the first time that he would prefer to be placed in foster care rather than return to his natural parents.
   To uncover the reasons why the boy dislikes his own home, of the following, it would be MOST advisable for you to

   A. ask the boy a number of short, simple questions about his feelings
   B. encourage the boy to talk freely and express his feelings as best he can
   C. interview the parents and find out why the boy doesn't want to live at home
   D. administer a battery of psychological tests in order to make an assessment of the boy's problems

   3.____

4. You are interviewing a mother who is applying for Aid to Families with Dependent Children because the husband has deserted the family. The mother becomes annoyed at having to answer your questions and tells you to leave her apartment.
   *Which one* of the following actions would be *most appropriate* to take FIRST in this situation?

   4.____

A. Return to the office and close the case for lack of cooperation
B. Tell the mother that you will get the information from her neighbors if she does not cooperate
C. Tell the mother that you must stay until you get answers to your questions
D. Explain to the mother the reasons for the interview and the consequences of Her failure to cooperate

5. A counselor counseling juvenile clients finds that, although he can tolerate most of their behavior, he becomes infuriated when they lie to him.
Of the following, the counselor can *BEST* deal with his anger at his clients' lying by

   A. recognizing his feelings of anger and learning to control expression of these feelings to his clients
   B. warning his clients that he cannot be responsible for his anger when a client lies to him
   C. using will power to suppress his feelings of anger when a client lies to him
   D. realizing that lying is a common trait of juveniles and not directed against him personally

6. During an interview, one of your clients, a former drug addict, has expressed an interest in attending a community counseling center and resuming his education.
In this case, the *MOST* appropriate action that you should take *FIRST* is to

   A. determine whether this ambition is realistic for a former drug addict
   B. send the client's application to a community counseling center which provides services to former addicts
   C. ask the client whether he is really motivated or is just seeking your approval
   D. encourage and assist the client to take this step, since his interest is a positive sign

7. You are interviewing a client who, during previous appointments, has not responded to your requests for information required to determine his continued eligibility for services. On this occasion, the client again offers an excuse which you feel is not acceptable.
For you to advise the client of the probable loss of services because of his lack of cooperation is

   A. *inappropriate,* because the threat to withhold services will harm the relationship between counselor and client
   B. *inappropriate,* because counselors should not reveal to clients that they do not believe their statements
   C. *appropriate,* because social services are a reward given to cooperative clients
   D. *appropriate,* beca,us.e the counselor should Inform clients of the consequences of their lack of cooperation

8. Assume that you are counselling an adolescent boy in a juvenile detention center who has been a ringleader in smuggling "pot" into the center.
During your regular interview with this boy, of the following, it would be *advisable* to

   A. tell him you know that he has been involved in smuggling pot and that you are trying to understand the reasons for his misbehavior
   B. ignore his pot smuggling in order to reassure him that you understand and accept him, even though you do not agree with his standards of behavior
   C. warn him that you have reported his pot smuggling and that he will be punished for his misbehavior
   D. show him that you disapprove of his pot smuggling, but assure him that you will not report him for his misbehavior

9. Your unit has received several complaints about a homeless elderly woman living outdoors in various locations in the area. To help determine the need for protective services for this woman, you interview several persons in the neighborhood who are familiar with her, but all are uncooperative or reluctant to give information.
Of the following, your *BEST* approach to these persons is to explain to them that

   A. you will take legal steps against them if they do not cooperate with you
   B. their cooperation may enable you to help this homeless woman
   C. you need their cooperation to remove this homeless woman from their neighborhood
   D. they will be responsible for any harm that comes to this homeless woman

10. Assume that you are interviewing a client regarding an adjustment in budget. The client begins to scream at you that she holds you responsible for the decrease in her allowance.
Of the following, *which* is the *BEST* way for you to handle this situation?

   A. Attempt to discuss the matter calmly with the client and explain her right to a hearing
   B. Urge the client to appeal and assure her of your support
   C. Tell the client that her disorderly behavior will be held against her
   D. Tell the client that the reduction is "due to red tape" and is not your fault

11. As a counselor assigned to a juvenile detention center, you are having a counselling interview with a recently admitted boy who is having serious problems in adjusting to confinement in the center. During the interview, the boy frequently interrupts to ask you personal questions. Of the following, the *BEST* way for you to deal with these questions is to

   A. tell him in a friendly way that your job is to discuss his problems, not yours
   B. try to understand how the questions relate to the boy's own problems and reply with discretion
   C. take no notice of the questions and continue with the interview
   D. try to win the boy's confidence by answering his questions in detail

12. A counselor is interviewing an elderly woman who hesitates to provide necessary information about her finances to determine whether she is eligible for supplementary assistance. She fears that this information will be reported to others and that her neighbors will find out that she is destitute and applying for "welfare." Of the following, the counselor's *MOST* appropriate response is to

   A. tell her that, if she hesitates to give this information, the agency will get it from other sources
   B. assure her that this information is kept strictly confidential and will not be given to unauthorized persons
   C. convince her that her application will be turned down unless she provides this information as soon as possible
   D. ask for the name and address of her nearest relative and obtain the information from that person

13. You are counseling a couple whose children have been placed in a foster home because of the couple's quarreling and child neglect. When you interview the wife by herself, she tells you that she knows the husband often "cheats" on her with other women, but she is too afraid of the husband's temper to tell him how much this hurts her.
For you to immediately reveal to the husband the wife's unhappiness concerning his "cheating" is, generally,

    A. *good practice,* because it will help the husband to understand why his wife quarrels with him
    B. *poor practice,* because information received from the wife should not be given to the husband without her permission
    C. *good practice,* because the husband will direct his anger at you rather than at his wife
    D. poor *practice,* because the wife may have told you a false story about her husband in order to win your sympathy

14. A counselor is beginning a job placement interview with a tall, strongly built young man. As the man sits down, the counselor comments: "I know a big fellow like you wouldn't be interested in any clerical job."
For the counselor to make such a comment is, generally,

    A. *appropriate,* because it creates an air of familiarity which may put the man at ease
    B. *inappropriate,* because the man may be sensitive about his physical size
    C. *appropriate,* because, the counselor is using his judgment to help speed up the interview
    D. *inappropriate,* because the man may feel he is being pressured into agreeing with the counselor

15. A counselor in a men's shelter is counseling a middle-aged client for alcoholism. During counseling, the" client confesses that, many years ago, he had often enjoyed sexually abusing his ten-year-old daughter. The counselor tells the client that he personally finds the client's behavior "morally disgusting."
For the counselor to tell the client this is, generally,

    A. *acceptable counseling practice,* because it may encourage the client to feel guilty about his behavior
    B. un*acceptable* cou*seling practice* , because the client may try to shock the counselor by confessing other similar behavior
    C. *acceptable counseling practice*, because "letting off steam" in this manner may relieve tension between the counselor and the client
    D. *unacceptable counseling practice,* because the client may hesitate to discuss his behavior frankly with the counselor in the future

16. During an interview, your client, who wants to move to a larger apartment, asks you to decide on a suitable neighborhood for her.
For you to make such a decision for the client would, generally, be considered

    A. *appropriate,* because you can save time and expense by sharing your knowledge of neighborhoods with the client
    B. *inappropriate,* because counselors should not help clients with this type of decision
    C. *appropriate,* because this will help the client to develop confidence in her ability to make decisions
    D. *inappropriate,* because the client should be encouraged to accept the responsibility of making this decision

17. A client tells you that he is extremely upset by the treatment that he received from Center personnel at the information desk.
Which of the following is the *BEST* way to handle this complaint during the interview?

    A. Explain to the client that he probably misinterpreted what occurred at the information desk
    B. Let the client express his feelings and then proceed with the interview
    C. Tell the client that you are not concerned with the personnel at the information desk
    D. Escort the client to the information desk to find out what really happened

18. You are finishing an interview with a client in which you have explained to her the procedure she must go through to apply for income maintenance.
Of the following, the *BEST* way for you to make sure that she has fully understood the procedure is to ask her

    A. whether she feels she has understood your explanation of the procedure
    B. whether she has any questions to ask you about the procedure
    C. to describe the procedure to you in her own words
    D. a few questions to test her understanding of the procedure

19. You are interviewing a client in his home as part of your investigation of an anonymous complaint that he has been receiving Medicaid fraudulently. During the interview, the client frequently interrupts your questions to discuss the hardships of his life and the bitterness he feels about his medical condition.
Of the following, the *BEST* way for you to deal with these discussions is to

    A. cut them off abruptly, since the client is probably just trying to avoid answering your questions
    B. listen patiently, since these discussions may be helpful to the client and may give you information for your investigation
    C. remind the client that you are investigating a complaint against him and he must answer directly
    D. seek to gain the client's confidence by discussing any personal or medical problems which you yourself may have

20. While interviewing an absent father to determine his ability to pay child supprt, you realize that his answers to some of your questions contradict his answers to other questions. Of the following, the BEST way for you to try to get accurate information from the father is to

    A. confront him with his contradictory answers and demand an explanation from him
    B. use your best judgment as to which of his answers are accurate and question him accordingly
    C. tell him that he has misunderstood your questions and that he must clarify his answers
    D. ask him the same questions in different words and follow up his answers with related questions

21. The one of the following types of interviewees who presents the LEAST difficult problem to handle is the person who

    A. answers with a great many qualifications
    B. talks at length about unrelated subjects so that the counselor cannot ask questions
    C. has difficulty understanding the counselor's vocabulary
    D. breaks into the middle of sentences and completes them with a meaning of his own

22. A man being interviewed is entitled to Medicaid, but he refuses to sign up for it because he says he cannot accept any form of welfare.
    Of the following, the BEST course of action to take FIRST is to

    A. try to discover the reason for his feeling this way
    B. tell him that he should be glad financial help is available
    C. explain that others cannot help him if he will not help himself
    D. suggest that he speak to someone who is already on Medicaid

23. Of the following, the outcome of an interview by a counselor depends MOST heavily on the

    A. personality of the interviewee
    B. personality of the counselor
    C. subject matter of the questions asked
    D. interaction between counselor and interviewee.

24. Some clients being interviewed are primarily interested in making a favorable impression. The counselor should be aware of the fact that such clients are *more likely* than other clients to

    A. try to anticipate the answers the interviewer is looking for
    B. answer all questions openly and frankly
    C. try to assume the role of interviewer
    D. be anxious to get the interview over as quickly as possible

25. The type of interview which a counselor usually conducts is substantially different from most interviewing situations in all of the following aspects EXCEPT the

    A. setting            B. kinds of clients
    C. techniques employed   D. kinds of problems

## KEY (CORRECT ANSWERS)

1. A
2. A
3. B
4. D
5. A

6. D
7. D
8. A
9. B
10. A

11. B
12. B
13. B
14. D
15. D

16. D
17. B
18. C
19. B
20. D

21. C
22. A
23. D
24. A
25. C

# EXAMINATION SECTION
## TEST 1

DIRECTIONS: Each question or incomplete statement is followed by several suggested answers or completions. Select the one that BEST answers the question or completes the statement. *PRINT THE LETTER OF THE CORRECT ANSWER IN THE SPACE AT THE RIGHT.*

1. One of the major objectives of a pre-employment interview is to get the interviewee to respond freely to inquiries.
   The one of the following actions that would be MOST likely to restrict the conversation of the interviewee would be for the investigator to
   A. keep a stenographic record of the interviewee's statements
   B. ask questions requiring complete explanations
   C. pose direct, specific questions to the interviewee
   D. allow the interviewee to respond to questions at his own pace

   1.\_\_\_\_

2. One of the reasons for the widespread use of the interview in personnel selection is that the interview
   A. has been shown to be a valid measurement technique
   B. is efficient and reliable
   C. has been demonstrated to result in consistency among raters
   D. allows for flexibility of response

   2.\_\_\_\_

3. In conducting a personnel interview, which of the following guidelines would be MOST desirable for the interviewer to follow?
   A. Allocate the same amount of time to each person being interviewed to standardize the process
   B. Ask exactly the same questions of all persons being interviewed to increase the objectivity of the process
   C. Eliminate the use of non-directive techniques because of their subjectivity
   D. Vary his style and technique to fit the purpose of the interview and the people being interviewed

   3.\_\_\_\_

4. You are planning to conduct preliminary interviews of applicants for an important position in your department.
   Which of the following planning considerations is LEAST likely to contribute to successful interviews?
   A. Make provisions to conduct interviews in privacy
   B. Schedule your appointments so that interviews will be short
   C. Prepare a list of your objectives
   D. Learn as much as you can about the applicant before the interview

   4.\_\_\_\_

5. When dealing with an aggrieved worker, a USEFUL interviewing technique is to
   A. maintain a sympathetic attitude
   B. maintain an attitude of cold impartiality

   5.\_\_\_\_

C. assure the subject that you are on his side
D. display a tape recorder to give the subject confidence that no parts of his story will be overlooked

6. The "patterned interview" is a device used by sophisticated employers to
   A. select employees who fit the ethnic pattern of the community
   B. ascertain the pattern of facts surrounding a grievance
   C. discourage workers from joining unions
   D. appraises a subject's most important character traits

6._____

7. One of the applicants for a menial job is a tall, stooped, husky individual with a low forehead, narrow eyes, a protruding chin, and a tendency to keep his mouth open.
In interviewing him, you should
   A. check him more carefully than the other applicants regarding criminal background
   B. disregard any skills he might have for other jobs which are vacant
   C. make your vocabulary somewhat simpler than with the other applicants
   D. make no assumptions regarding his ability on the basis of his appearance

7._____

8. Of the following, the BEST approach for you to use at the beginning of an interview with a job applicant is to
   A. caution him to use his time economically and to get to the point
   B. ask him how long he intends to remain on the job if hired
   C. make some pleasant remarks to put him at ease
   D. emphasize the importance of the interview in obtaining the job

8._____

9. Of the following, the BEST reason for conducting an "exit interview" with an employee is to
   A. make certain that he returns all identification cards and office keys
   B. find out why he is leaving
   C. provide a useful training device for the exit interviewer
   D. discover if his initial hiring was in error

9._____

10. If you are to interview several applicants for jobs and rate them on five different factors on a scale of 1 to 5, you should be MOST careful to *insure* that your
    A. rating on one factor does not influence your rating on another factor
    B. ratings on all factors are interrelated with a minimum of variation
    C. overall evaluation for employment exactly reflects the arithmetic average of your ratings
    D. overall evaluation for employment is unrelated to your individual ratings

10._____

11. Of the following, the question MOST appropriate for initial screening purposes GENERALLY is:
    A. What are your salary requirements?
    B. Why do you think you would like this kind of work?
    C. How did you get along with your last supervisor?
    D. What are your vocational goals?

11._____

12. Of the following, normally the question MOST appropriate for selection purposes generally would tend to be:
    A. Where did you work last?
    B. When did you graduate from high school?
    C. What was your average in school?
    D. Why did you select this organization?

13. Assume that you have been asked to interview each of several students who have been hired to work part-time.
    Which of the following would ordinarily be accomplished LEAST effectively in such an interview?
    A. Providing information about the organization or institution in which the students will be working
    B. Directing the students to report for work each afternoon at specified times
    C. Determining experience and background of the students so that appropriate assignments can be made
    D. Changing the attitudes of the students toward the importance of parental controls

14. In interviewing job applicants, which of the following usually does NOT have to be done before the end of the interview?
    A. Making a decision to hire an applicant
    B. Securing information from applicants
    C. Giving information to applicants
    D. Establishing a friendly relationship with applicants

15. In the process of interviewing applicants for a position on your staff, the one of the following which would be BEST is to
    A. make sure all applicants are introduced to the other members of your staff prior to the formal interview
    B. make sure the applicant does not ask questions about the job or the department
    C. avoid having the applicant talk with the staff at the conclusion of a successful interview
    D. introduce applicants to some of the staff at the conclusion of a successful interview

16. While interviewing a job applicant, you ask applicant why he left his last job. The applicant does not answer immediately.
    Of the following, the BEST action to take at that point is to
    A. wait until he answers
    B. ask another question
    C. repeat the question in a loud voice
    D. ask him why he does not answer

17. You know that a student applying for a job in your office has done well in college except for two courses in science. However, when you ask him about his grades, his reply is vague and general.

It would be BEST for you to
- A. lead the applicant to admitting doing poorly in science to be sure that the facts are correct
- B. judge the applicant's tact and skill in handling what may be for him a personally sensitive question
- C. immediately confront the applicant with the facts and ask for an explanation
- D. ignore the applicant's response since you have the transcript

18. A college student has applied for a position with your department. Prior to conducting an interview of the job applicant, it would be LEAST helpful for you to have
    - A. a personal resume
    - B. a job description
    - C. references
    - D. hiring requirements

19. Job applicants tend to be nervous during interviews.
    Which of the following techniques is MOST likely to put such an applicant at ease?
    - A. Try to establish rapport by asking general questions which are easily answered by the applicant
    - B. Ask the applicant to describe his career objectives immediately, thus minimizing the anxiety caused by waiting
    - C. Start the interview with another member of the staff present so that the applicant does not feel alone
    - D. Proceed as rapidly as possible, since the emotional state of the applicant is none of your concern

20. At the first interview between a supervisor and a newly appointed subordinate, GREATEST care should be taken to
    - A. build toward a satisfactory personal relationship even if some other objectives of the interview must be postponed
    - B. cover a predetermined list of specific objectives so as to make a further orientation interview unnecessary
    - C. create an image of a forceful, determined supervisor whose wishes cannot be opposed by a subordinate without great risk
    - D. create an impression of efficiency and control of operation free from interpersonal relationships

21. You are a supervisor in an agency and are holding your first interview with a new employee.
    In this interview, you should strive MAINLY to
    - A. show the new employee that you are an efficient and objective supervisor, with a completely impersonal attitude toward your subordinates
    - B. complete the entire orientation process including the giving of detailed job-duty instructions

C. make it clear to the employee that all your decisions are based on your many years of experience
D. lay the groundwork for a good employee-supervisor relationship by gaining the new employee's confidence

22. The INCORRECT statement related to the principles of interviewing is:
    A. Written outlines should be avoided by the interviewer because they tend to be overly restrictive.
    B. Preliminary planning (for the interview) should involve an analysis of the point of view of the person to be interviewed.
    C. An interviewing supervisor should make every effort to conduct it in privacy to avoid possible inhibitions.
    D. Well-planned questions are sometimes necessary in conducting an interview.

22.____

23. Assume that you are conducting an interview with a prospective employee who is of limited mental ability and low socio-economic status.
    Of the following, it is MOST likely that asking him many open-ended questions about his work experience would cause him to respond
    A. articulately    B. reluctantly    C. comfortably    D. aggressively

23.____

24. An individual interview is to be used as part of an examination for a supervisory position.
    Of the following, the attribute or characteristic that is LEAST suitable for evaluation in such an interview is
    A. ability to supervise people      B. poise and confidence
    C. response to stress conditions    D. rigidity and flexibility

24.____

25. In conducting a disciplinary interview, a supervisor finds that he must ask some highly personal questions which are relevant to the problem at hand.
    The interviewer is MOST likely to get TRUTHFUL answers to these questions if he asks them
    A. early in the interview, before the interviewee has had a chance to become emotional
    B. in a manner so that the interviewee can answer them with a simple "yes" or "no"
    C. well into the interview, after rapport and trust have been established
    D. just after the close of the interview, so that the questions appear to be off the record

25.____

## KEY (CORRECT ANSWERS)

| | | | | |
|---|---|---|---|---|
| 1. | A | | 11. | A |
| 2. | D | | 12. | D |
| 3. | D | | 13. | D |
| 4. | B | | 14. | A |
| 5. | A | | 15. | D |
| | | | | |
| 6. | D | | 16. | A |
| 7. | D | | 17. | B |
| 8. | C | | 18. | C |
| 9. | B | | 19. | A |
| 10. | A | | 20. | A |

21. D
22. A
23. B
24. A
25. C

# TEST 2

DIRECTIONS: Each question or incomplete statement is followed by several suggested answers or completions. Select the one that BEST answers the question or completes the statement. *PRINT THE LETTER OF THE CORRECT ANSWER IN THE SPACE AT THE RIGHT.*

1. Of the following methods of conducting an interview, the BEST is to
    A. ask questions with "yes" or "no" answers
    B. listen carefully and ask only questions that are pertinent
    C. fire questions at the interviewee so that he must answer sincerely and briefly
    D. read standardized questions to the person being interviewed

2. An interviewer should begin with topics which are easy to talk about and which are not threatening.
   This procedure is useful MAINLY because it
    A. allows the applicant a little time to get accustomed to the situation and leads to freer communication
    B. distracts the attention of the person being interviewed from the main purpose of the questioning
    C. is the best way for the interviewer to show that he is relaxed and confident on the job
    D. causes the interviewee to feel that the interviewer is apportioning valuable questioning time

3. The initial interview will normally be more of a problem to the interviewer than any subsequent interviews he may have with the same person because
    A. the interviewee is likely to be hostile
    B. there is too much to be accomplished in one session
    C. he has less information about the client than he will have later
    D. some information may be forgotten when later making record of this first interview

4. Most successful interviews are those in which the interviewer shows a genuine interest in the person he is questioning.
   This attitude would MOST likely cause the individual being interviewed to
    A. feel that the interviewer already knows all the facts in his case
    B. act more naturally and reveal more of his true feelings
    C. request that the interviewer give more attention to his problems, not his personality
    D. react defensively, suppress his negative feelings and conceal the real facts in his case

5. When interviewing a person, the interviewer may easily slip into error in rating his subject's personal qualities because of the general impression he receives of the individual.
   This tendency is known as the
    A. "halo" effect            B. subjective bias problem
    C. "person-to-person" error  D. inflation effect

6. An interviewer would find an interview checklist LEAST useful for
   A. making sure that all the principal facts are secured in the interview
   B. insuring that the claimant's grievance is settled in his favor
   C. facilitating later research into the nature of the problems handled by the agency
   D. conducting the interview in a logical and orderly fashion

7. There are almost as many techniques of interviewing as there are interviews. Of the following, the LEAST objectionable method is to
   A. ask if interviewee minds being quoted
   B. make occasional notes as important topics some up
   C. take notes unobtrusively
   D. take shorthand notes of every word

8. Questions worded so that the person being interviewed has some hint of the desired answer can modify the person's response.
   The result of the inclusion of such questions in an interview, even when they ae used inadvertently, is to
   A. have no effect on the basic content of the information given by the person interviewed
   B. have value in convincing the person that the suggested plan is the best for him
   C. cause the person to give more meaningful information
   D. reduce the validity of the meaningful information obtained from the person

9. The person MOST likely to be a good interviewer is one who
   A. is able to outguess the person being interviewed
   B. tries to change the attitudes of the persons he interviews
   C. controls the interview by skillfully dominating the conversation
   D. is able to imagine himself in the position of the person being interviewed

10. The "halo effect" is an overall impression on the interviewee, whether favorable or unfavorable, usually created by a single trait. This impression then influences the appraisal of all other factors.
    A "halo effect" is LEAST likely to be created at an interview where the interviewee is a
    A. person of average appearance and ability
    B. rough-looking man who uses abusive language
    C. young attractive woman being interviewed by a man
    D. person who demonstrates an exceptional ability to remember faces

11. Of the following, the BEST way for an interviewer to calm a person who seems to have become emotionally upset as a result of a question asked is for the interviewer to
    A. talk to the person about other things for a short time
    B. ask that the person control himself
    C. probe for the cause of his emotional upset
    D. finish the questioning as quickly as possible

12. Of the following, the GREATEST pitfall in interviewing is that the result may be affected by the
    A. bias of the interviewee
    B. bias of the interviewer
    C. educational level of the interviewee
    D. educational level of the interviewer

13. Assume you are assigned to interview applicants.
    Of the following, which is the BEST attitude for you to take in dealing with applicants?
    A. Assume they will enjoy being interviewed because they believe that you have the power of decision
    B. Expect that they have a history of anti-social behavior in the family, and probe deeply into the social development of family members
    C. Expect that they will try to control the interview, thus you should keep them on the defensive
    D. Assume that they will be polite and cooperative and attempt to secure the information you need in a business-like manner

14. A Spanish-speaking applicant may want to bring his bilingual child with him to an interview to act as an interpreter.
    Which of the following would be LEAST likely to affect the value of an interview in which an applicant's child has acted as interpreter?
    A. It may make it undesirable to ask certain questions.
    B. A child may do an inadequate job of interpretation.
    C. A child's answers may indicate his feelings toward his parents.
    D. The applicant may not want to reveal all information in front of his child.

15. In answering questions asked by students, faculty, and the public, it is MOST important that
    A. you indicate your source of information
    B. you are not held responsible for the answers
    C. the facts you give be accurate
    D. the answers cover every possible aspect of each question

16. Assume that someone you are interviewing is reluctant to give you certain information.
    He would probably be MORE responsive if you show him that
    A. all the other persons you interviewed provided you with the information
    B. it would serve his own best interests to give you the information
    C. the information is very important to you
    D. you are business-like and take a no-nonsense approach

17. Taking notes while you are interviewing someone is MOST likely to
    A. arouse doubts as to your trustworthiness
    B. give the interviewee confidence in your ability
    C. insure that you record the facts you think are important
    D. make the responses of the interviewee unreliable

18. In developing a role-playing situation to be used to train interviewers, the one of the following that it would be MOST important to use as a guide is that the situation
    A. allow the role player to identify readily with the role he is to play
    B. be free of actual or potential conflict between the role players
    C. can be clearly recognized by the participants as an actual interview situation that has already taken place
    D. should provide a detailed set of specifications for handling the roles to be played

19. Restating a question before the person being interviewed gives an answer to the original question is usually NOT good practice principally because
    A. the client will think that you don't know your job
    B. it may confuse the client
    C. the interviewer should know exactly what to ask and how to put the question
    D. it reveals the interviewer's insecurity

20. In interviewing a man who has a grievance, it is IMPORTANT that the interviewer
    A. take note of such physical responses as shifty eyes
    B. use a lie detector, if possible, to ascertain the truth in doubtful situations
    C. allow the complainant to "tell his story"
    D. place the complainant under oath

21. Ideally, the setting for an interview should NOT include
    A. an informal opening        B. privacy and comfort
    C. an atmosphere of leisure   D. a lie detector

22. Which of the following is an example of a "non-directive" interview?
    A. The subject directs his remarks at someone other than the interviewer.
    B. The subject discusses any topics that seem to be relevant to him.
    C. The subject has not been directed that he need answer any particular questions.
    D. The interview is confined to the facts of the case and is not directed at eliciting personal information.

23. Of the following abilities, the one which is LEAST important in conducting an interview is the ability to
    A. ask the interviewee pertinent questions
    B. evaluate the interviewee on the basis of appearance
    C. evaluate the responses of the interviewee
    D. gain the cooperation of the interviewee

24. Which of the following actions would be LEAST desirable for you to take when you have to conduct an interview?
    A. Set a relaxed and friendly atmosphere
    B. Plan your interview ahead of time
    C. Allow the person interviewed to structure the interview as he wishes
    D. Include some stock or standard question which you ask everyone.

25. One of the MOST important techniques for conducting good interviews is
    A. asking the applicant questions in rapid succession, thereby keeping the conversation properly focused
    B. listening carefully to all that the applicant has to say, making mental notes of possible areas for follow-up
    C. indicating to the applicant the criteria and standards on which you will base your judgment
    D. making sure that you are interrupted about five minutes before you wish to end so that you can keep on schedule

## KEY (CORRECT ANSWERS)

1. B
2. A
3. C
4. B
5. A

6. B
7. C
8. D
9. D
10. A

11. A
12. B
13. D
14. C
15. C

16. B
17. C
18. A
19. B
20. C

21. D
22. B
23. B
24. C
25. B

# BASIC FUNDAMENTALS OF INTERVIEWING

## TABLE OF CONTENTS

| | Page |
|---|---|
| INSTRUCTIONAL OBJECTIVES | 1 |
| CONTENT | 1 |
| INTRODUCTION | 1 |
| 1. Before the Interview Starts | 1 |
|     Reasons for Interviews | 1 |
|     Completing Applications or Forms | 2 |
| 2. Conducting Interviews | 2 |
|     Starting the Interview | 2 |
|     Importance of Understanding People | 3 |
|     Guiding the Body of the Interview | 3 |
|     Related Factors | 3 |
|     Purpose of Interview | 3 |
|     Closing the Interview | 4 |
|     Remembering Key Points | 4 |
|     Problems in Interviewing | 4 |
| 3. After the Interview | 6 |
|     Evaluating the Interview | 6 |
|     Checking References | 7 |
|     Obtaining Information from References | 7 |
| STUDENT LEARNING ACTIVITIES | 8 |
| TEACHER MANAGEMENT ACTIVITIES | 8 |
| EVALUATION QUESTIONS | 9 |
|     Answer Key | 11 |

# BASIC FUNDAMENTALS OF INTERVIEWING

## INSTRUCTIONAL OBJECTIVES

1. Ability of the public-service employee to work toward becoming a good interviewer or interviewee on his job and in his life
2. Ability to conduct referral or other interviews to obtain and verify information
3. Ability to observe interviewees skillfully
4. Ability to evaluate the effectiveness of an interview
5. Ability to cope with problems that come up during an interview
6. Ability to check an applicant's references

## CONTENT

INTRODUCTION

This unit is designed to develop the student's ability to interview people, and to obtain and verify information. It will also give trainees practice in special-purpose interviews, such as making referrals, classifying prohibited behavior, protective intervention, employment, financial eligibility, etc.

Public-service workers will be required to give different kinds of interviews on various occasions. They may be required to interview other professional personnel in their major occupational group and to grant interviews to official personnel. They will certainly be interviewed at some time for such things as jobs, raises, credit ratings, and opening bank accounts. Certain public-service workers will also be required to interview clients, patients, pupils, families, etc.

For the majority of the students, the role of an interviewer will be a new one. In the past, some of them have been the unwilling, nervous, perhaps hostile recipients of interviews by welfare workers, police, and employers. Practice interviews, relative to their future jobs, can serve as a base for proficiency in interviewing skills.

Students should acquire necessary theory and skills to become aware of the various kinds of interviews and the people who conduct them. Various types of interviews include: employment, counseling, newspaper reporting and police interrogation. Interviews are performed by a wide variety of people: psychologists, social-service workers, lawyers, salesmen, policemen, tax inspectors, immigration officers, journalists, and many more.

1. BEFORE THE INTERVIEW STARTS

Reasons for Interviews: The kind of interview depends basically on its reason – some give advice, some seek information, some give information. Here are some of the major reasons for conducting an interview:
- To obtain information
- To evaluate a person's background
- To evaluate the interviewee's character and/or personality

- To provide information
- To maintain good public or employee relations

<u>Completing Applications or Forms:</u> Another major reason for conducting an interview is to help the public or coworkers in filling out applications or forms. In this kind of interview one needs to assist the interviewee in clarifying needed information or in filling in the form correctly. Since needed information can easily be omitted, the forms must be checked for completeness.

If a form is to be used for a later interview, the interviewer may want to prepare questions from the information furnished. Areas to look for in this case include:
- Identifying factors needing elaboration
- Identifying factors that will bring out more information
- Identifying factors that are not clear

In reviewing applications or forms, there are certain critical areas to watch for, such as an interviewee's work experience. The applicant's work experience should contain sufficient details in these areas:

- Amounts of time
- Types of work experience
- Financial levels of compensation

These three factors are usually given great weight in evaluating the applicant. Other important areas to watch include the applicant's financial ability, and his prior credit references. Age should be taken into account when checking credit references. A young man or woman, for example, should not be expected to have established an extensive credit rating.

## 2. CONDUCTING INTERVIEWS

*An interview is essentially an interaction between people through words and acts. During this process, knowledge is acquired by both interviewer and interviewee.*

It is important to note that the information sought should be purposeful and related to the reason for the interview. A license interviewer should not be primarily concerned with attempting to classify whether the interviewee's behavior requires intervention from the law enforcement agencies. Common sense should dictate that the kinds of questions asked should be determined by the "role" of the agency, and the immediate concerns of the person being interviewed.

<u>Starting the Interview:</u> One of the first tasks in the beginning of an interview is the establishment of rapport, or mutual liking or respect. After a friendly atmosphere has been created by putting the applicant at ease, the interviewer can ask the first question. If the interview has to do with a specific application, the interviewer should pick non-controversial matter from the form to discuss first. Use of these techniques is designed to get the applicant talking. An atmosphere should be created that will encourage the interviewee to discuss freely what is on his mind.

Importance of Understanding People: The interviewer should have a good knowledge of human behavior and interpersonal relationships. He should realize that people often behave in an inconsistent way. They may give themselves away in an interview by saying one thing orally, and by expressing the opposite meaning in body movements.

The interviewer should be able to observe applicants skillfully. The responsibility of utilizing all the senses to obtain and mentally verify information received during the interview occurs daily on the job. The successful social-service worker, for example, must master these techniques quickly in order to improve his effectiveness.

Guiding the Body of the Interview: Ask questions to get information. There are basically two kinds of questions: *directive* and *nondirective.*

The *directive question,* as its name implies, guides or directs the interviewee in a specific area. Directive questions can usually be answered with a few words, such as "yes" or "no." A typical directive question might be, "How long have you worked at the XYZ Company?"

*Nondirective questions,* on the other hand, give the interviewee a chance to say what is on his mind. Words such as *what, how,* and *why* are often used in nondirective questioning. A typical nondirective question might be, "Why did you leave the XYZ Company, Mr. Rean?"

A good technique to use to encourage the applicant to talk is to begin with a nondirective question. If the applicant does not respond appropriately to a nondirective question, then use a more directive question. An example of this technique could be:

Interviewer: *What did you dislike most about your last job?*
Interviewee: *Oh, not much.*
Interviewer: *Did you feel as though your supervisor treated you fairly?*
Interviewee: *My supervisor! That guy was definitely not fair – let me tell you...*

In the above simplified example one can see how the interviewer began with a general question about the job, and when he felt that the applicant didn't respond appropriately, he used a more specific directive question, which in this case triggered a response from the applicant. By alternating between directive and nondirective questions, an interviewer can skillfully guide the discussion and obtain the necessary information from the interviewee.

Related Factors: Factors that will affect the relationship in the interview can either help or hinder the process. These will strengthen the relationship: interest, demonstrated concern, attentiveness, willingness to listen, and questioning for fuller understanding of issues at hand. On the other hand, there are some factors which obstruct relationships, such as indifference, judgmental attitudes, insensitivity, being aloof, inactivity, or being late for appointments.

Purpose of Interview: If the purpose of the interview is to help the interviewee, the interviewer should be *supportive,* and exhibit a positive and active understanding of feelings which are given expression by his behavior. However, if the interview is designed to be an interrogation of a prisoner, the method of its conduct is determined by many factors: suspect, crime, time element, and location (field, home, or headquarters).

Techniques and methods of police interrogation have had to change in recent years, and the police must now be more aware of protecting each citizen's private rights. Each suspect should be advised of his rights before his statement will be considered admissible for evidence. Citizens must not be arbitrarily subjected to interrogation; the officer must have more than just a hunch, and must be able to substantiate his reason for an interrogation. However, if an officer has good reason to be suspicious, whatever the reasons may be, he has a duty to make the inquiry or interrogation.

As can be seen, the purpose of the interview can have a drastic effect on guiding the body of the interview.

Closing the Interview: In terminating the interview, the interviewee should be told when he can expect a decision or obtain the necessary information he needs. If possible, the interviewer should answer any final questions the applicant may have.

If the applicant has to be rejected, the interviewer should accomplish this diplomatically. Courtesy and tact are especially important at this point in the interview, if a good image of the interviewer's agency is to be projected to the public.

If the interview had definite time limits, it is a good idea to remind the applicant at the beginning of this fact, and once again a few minutes before the time is up, to give the interviewee a chance to conclude his discourse.

Remembering Key Points: An effective technique for the interviewer to use during the interview is to take notes. This will help him to remember the main points of the conversation. On some occasions, however, taking notes during the course of an interview can be distracting to the applicant, or can sometimes inhibit the interviewee's responsiveness. In such cases, the interviewer should write his notes immediately after the interview. The applicant will not then be distracted, and the interviewer can remember the key points of the discussion while they are still fresh in his mind.

Problems in Interviewing: A major difficulty in interviewing involves dealing with *ambivalence* (feelings of simultaneous attraction and repulsion) and sometimes, open conflict. The interviewer should become aware of these types of applicant behavior:

- The person asks for advice, but doesn't use it
- The person agrees to a plan, but doesn't carry it out
- The person says one thing, and does another

Does this ambivalence exist in only the interviewee, or does it also exist in the interviewer? In fact, the degree to which the interviewer understands himself and is aware of his own feelings has a direct effect on the conduct of the interview. Problem areas to explore include:

- *The feelings of the Interviewer* – Do they interfere in an interview? What forms of expression do they take? Is control of one's own feelings important? Why?
- *Over-involvement by the Interviewer* – Is this helpful or harmful? What kinds of behavior might result from a non-professional approach to interviewing?

*Prejudice:* If the interviewer is rigid and inflexible in his thinking, this could have a harmful impact on the interview. The goal of the interviewer should be to become aware of his personal biases, and honestly try to control them, so that the interview can be conducted in a fair and honest way.

*Confidentiality:* A public office is, in many ways, a public trust. As an interviewer, one should become familiar with the extent to which confidential information is shared by other people in his agency. The procedures for sharing confidential information should be known, and a clear definition should be given at each agency as to what constitutes confidential information. Whenever information of a confidential nature must be shared with others, it should be on a need-to-know basis, and its confidentiality should be carefully explained to the person receiving the information.

*Dependence, Interdependence and Independence:*

- How are the qualities of dependence, interdependence and independence manifested in the interview? To some extent, these characteristics exist in all people.
- Are these qualities good or bad, or does it depend upon the circumstances?

For example, a positive aspect of dependence is the ability to trust and form deep personal relationships. A negative aspect of being overly dependent is the resultant lack of self-reliance and initiative. People who are independent are usually self-confident; however, too much independence could be a problem in the interviewing process. Interdependence among individuals can be seen in marriages, working relationships, and in interviewing. Examples of group interdependences include:

- Between agencies
- Between agencies and the community, and
- Between local, state and federal governmental agencies

*Undue Hurry When Questioning Applicants:*

- Don't anticipate what the interviewee is going to say. It's easy to jump to conclusions; much harder to hold one's judgment.
- Another habit to avoid is putting words in the applicant's mouth.
- Don't let the applicant lead you astray in the interview.
- Get the interviewee back on the track by acknowledging his remark, and asking a directive question back on the main point of the discussion.

*Controlling the Interview:* The extent to which the interviewer feels a need to control the interview will, of course, be determined by the purpose of the interview. Much less control would be exerted on an interviewee in a social-service agency than in a law enforcement agency while interrogating a suspect.

Shy applicants should be encouraged to open up by asking them non-directive or open-ended questions. An overly talkative applicant can be controlled by asking more directive questions, and by watching for digressions during the discussion.

*Common Weaknesses of Interviewers:* Here are some of the more common faults of interviewers:

- *Talking too much* – especially in those interviews that are designed to get information from the interviewee.
- *Guiding applicant too much* – particularly in those interviews that are designed to allow the interviewee to express whatever is troubling him.
- *Dominating the interview* – it should be a process of give and take.
- *Talking down to the applicant* – this condescending attitude can usually be spotted pretty easily.
- *Failing to listen* – a common fault, however, inexcusable for an interviewer.

## 3. AFTER THE INTERVIEW

### Evaluating the Interview

- What information was learned about the applicant?
- Was it sufficient?
- What was not learned that should have been?
- If problems came up in the interview, who made the decisions?
- What was the role of the interviewer and interviewee?

Some of the factors involved in decision-making are:

- Facts involved – how are they maintained?
- Availability of acceptable alternatives
- Readiness to take action

There are definite dangers to be aware of when making decisions or evaluating an interviewee. One such danger is irrational prejudice. Each of us is biased to a certain extent, either for or against certain ethnic, racial, or religious groups. The better the interviewer understands himself, and In particular the more he is aware of his personal beliefs towards certain individuals and groups, the better off he will be for having recognized them. He can then compensate for any prejudicial bias.

This bias could work in the opposite manner. For example, an interviewer could be so blinded by an applicant's good traits, that he would not see his faults because of this *halo effect*.

Checking References: A part of the process of many interviews involves the actual checking of personal references for these purposes:

- To verify information obtained from the application and interview
- To obtain an evaluation by people who know the interviewee's work history
- To obtain additional information not disclosed on the application or during the interview

Additional verifying information may be obtained from letters of reference supplied by the applicant. There are some disadvantages to letters of reference. They may be vague or even dishonest. Sometimes, such letters may not contain the information sought. Quite often, information supplied directly by the applicant's past employers is the best source to use. When evaluating replies, consider these factors:

- They may not be complete
- They may be vague to cover negative factors
- They may contain information taken from records which may not tell the complete story

Obtaining Information from References: Letter writing is a standard way of obtaining information about an individual. However since a letter may take too much time, or cost too much, it is recommended that the telephone should be used whenever possible. One reason for the telephone's effectiveness is that a direct contact with the reference is possible. This makes for better communication, since specific questions and follow-up answers can be obtained. In addition, doubts and omissions can be picked up from the person's voice.

Before making a telephone call to a reference, a checklist of questions should first be prepared. In talking to the reference, the following guidelines should be utilized.

- Establish rapport
- Be businesslike
- Let reference talk freely
- Don't put words in respondent's mouth
- Probe for strengths and weaknesses

A personal visit is sometimes advantageous, and can often be more effective in bringing out more information about the applicant. In such cases, arrange to meet the reference and use the same principles as in the telephone checks.

Finally, information may be obtained concerning references by the hiring of outside investigators. This method has the advantages of getting more personal and more objective information. There are, however certain disadvantages: the outside investigator may not obtain the best available information, and there may be considerable expense involved.

## STUDENT LEARNING ACTIVITIES

- Participate in role-playing exercises after being given a brief introduction to the basic techniques of interviewing.
- Role-play in a wide variety of interviews, such as employment, welfare eligibility, and license application, and gain experience as both an interviewer and interviewee.
- Observe interviews during role-playing exercises, evaluating what the interviewee is communicating.
- Listen to examples of interviews on tape, and be prepared to discuss the techniques used to overcome problems that developed during the interview.
- Interview public-service workers in your community about their jobs to learn more about careers, and practice newly acquired interviewing skills.
- Write a short essay on how to conduct an interview. Include the start, guidance, conclusion, and evaluation of the results.
- Talk to public-service employees who do a great deal of interviewing in their jobs. Be prepared to discuss questions with them.
- Talk to your school guidance counselor or psychologist about interviewing skills.

## TEACHER MANAGEMENT ACTIVITIES

- Plan on utilizing role-playing exercises to practice knowledge learned.
- Have students play both the interviewer and interviewee in various types of interviews, such as eligibility, employment, license interviews, etc.
- Prepare tapes of different types of interviews, and play them for the class to discuss and evaluate.
- Encourage students to use all their senses as interviewers to carefully observe what is being communicated by the interviewee.
- Encourage individual practice of interviewing skills whenever possible, such as with local public-service employees.
- Assign short essays on the process of interviewing: starting, guiding, concluding, and evaluating.
- Obtain specialized interviewing materials, such as public-safety techniques from neighboring police departments.
- Arrange to have public service workers come into the class to talk about interviewing techniques.
- Provide opportunities for the school guidance counselor or psychologist to discuss interviewing skills.
- Approach the theory of interviewing through practice situations whenever possible.
- Borrow interviewing films from the local library or educational resource center.

## Evaluation Questions
## Interviewing Skills

1. The purpose of an interview could be:　　　　　　　　　　　　　　　　1._____
    - A. To obtain information
    - B. To give information
    - C. To evaluate a person's background
    - D. All of the above

2. The first job of the interview is to:　　　　　　　　　　　　　　　　2._____
    - A. Get to the subject quickly
    - B. Put the applicant at ease
    - C. Tell the applicant about the boss
    - D. Tell the applicant about the job that is open

3. A skillful interview will:　　　　　　　　　　　　　　　　3._____
    - A. Watch the applicant's body language
    - B. Listen to the applicant
    - C. Ask questions to get information
    - D. All of the above

4. Questions that are specific and can be answered "yes" or "no" are:　　4._____
    - A. Directive
    - B. Non-directive
    - C. Indirective
    - D. None of the above

5. If the applicant cannot be hired, the interview should:　　　　　　5._____
    - A. Avoid telling the applicant
    - B. Tell the applicant as bluntly as possible
    - C. Tell the applicant tactfully
    - D. Give the applicant another chance

6. Taking notes during an interview can:　　　　　　　　　　　　6._____
    - A. Help the interviewer remember the main points
    - B. Be distracting to the interviewee
    - C. Make the interviewee reluctant to talk
    - D. All of the above

7. An interviewer with personal likes and dislikes should:　　　　　　7._____
    - A. Try to control them in order to be flexible
    - B. Try to find people with the same likes and dislikes
    - C. Try to get rid of all personal likes and dislikes
    - D. None of the above

8. The telephone is an effective way of finding information because        8._____
    A. Doubts can be picked up from a person's voice
    B. The person called can talk freely
    C. It doesn't take much time
    D. All of the above

9. Interviewers should:        9._____
    A. Reach conclusions about the applicant as soon as possible
    B. Keep applicants on track by asking directive questions
    C. Let applicants talk on any subject comfortable to them
    D. Help with words when the applicant is unable to think

10. Shy applicants may talk more if the interviewer:        10._____
    A. Looks bored
    B. Asks open-ended questions
    C. Asks directive questions
    D. Does most of the talking

11. Interviewers should:        11._____
    A. Talk down to the applicant
    B. Make sure they dominate the interview
    C. Listen as well as talk
    D. Guide the applicant's words

12. After interviews, interviewers should ask themselves:        12._____
    A. What was learned about the applicant?
    B. What was not learned?
    C. What problems came up and if they were solved?
    D. All of the above

13. Which one is not a reason for asking for personal references?        13._____
    A. To find out information about the applicant's family
    B. To find what people who know the applicant think of their work
    C. To find out if the information on the application is true
    D. To get more information

14. Letters of reference may be:        14._____
    A. Incomplete
    B. Vague
    C. Dishonest
    D. All of the above

15. Information told in confidence should:        15._____
    A. Not be kept from all office personnel
    B. Not be told to anyone
    C. Be told to those who need-to-know
    D. None of the above

## KEY (CORRECT ANSWERS)

| | | |
|---|---|---|
| 1. D | 6. D | 11. C |
| 2. B | 7. A | 12. D |
| 3. D | 8. D | 13. A |
| 4. A | 9. B | 14. D |
| 5. C | 10. B | 15. C |

# BASIC FUNDAMENTALS OF INTERVIEWING AND COUNSELING

## CONTENTS

| | Page |
|---|---|
| I. INTRODUCTION | 1 |
| II. PRESENTATION | 1 |
|     A. The Art of Interviewing | 1 |
|     B. Types of Interviews | 1 |
|         1. Classified by Purpose | 1 |
|         2. Classified by Method | 3 |
|         3. Classified by Technique | 3 |
|     C. How to Conduct Interviews | 3 |
|         1. Preparing for the Interview | 3 |
|         2. Conducting the Interview | 4 |
|         3. Closing the Interview | 5 |
|     D. The Counseling Interview | 6 |
|         1. Purpose of Counseling Interviews | 6 |
|         2. The Supervisor as a Counselor | 6 |
|     E. Interview Checklist | 7 |
| III. SUMMARY | 8 |
| Sample Questions | 9 |
| Interviewing and Counseling – Outlines 1-5 | 10 |

86

# INTERVIEWING AND COUNSELING

I. **INTRODUCTION**

For this unit, our objectives are limited. Both interviewing and counseling have been, and are now, the subjects of extensive study. Advances in knowledge in these fields occur from day-to-day. All that we can hope to accomplish is to give you an overview that will help you to more effectively use the interview, including the counseling interview, in meeting your supervisory responsibilities. We will discuss, generally, what an interview is, the various types of interviews, and how to conduct interviews.

Our objectives are to provide you with: (1) an understanding of the art of interviewing, (2) knowledge of the uses of interviews, and (3) knowledge of techniques for successfully conducting interviews and counseling.

II. **PRESENTATION**

A. The Art of Interviewing

Interviewing is an art. It is more than a systematized body of knowledge. To be a successful interviewer, one has to develop skill in handling an interview situation. Because the interview takes place between two or more human beings, highly individualized, with differing emotional responses, no set of rules can be applicable at all times in all situations. It is the discernment of the right approach to any given interview situation which gives rise to the art.

You are not strangers to interviewing. You have all been interviewed at one time or another. It is probably safe to say that all of you have conducted interviews. Having been on both sides of the interviewing situation, you have recognized that the emotional responses of the interviewer and interviewee differ. You have, perhaps, felt that if the person interviewing you knew what he was doing, you would derive more from the interview. Or while interviewing, you may have wondered how the interview got out of hand, or why the interviewee reacted as he did. If so, you may have become aware of the fact that an interview involves a subtler relationship between human beings than is commonly supposed.

What, then, is an interview? It is a purposeful, directed conversation between two or more people. It is not an aimless conversation. It has a definite purpose, and the conversation is directed toward accomplishing that purpose. The person who takes the responsibility for the direction of the conversation is the interviewer.

What are the purposes for which interviews are intended? Generally speaking, these purposes are: (1) to obtain information, (2) to give information, (3) to solve problems, and (4) to influence the behavior of individuals. An interview may combine two or more purposes. To discuss these purposes more fully, let us look at the types of interviews.

B. Types of Interviews
  1. Classified By Purpose
     a. Fact Finding Interviews
        This type of interview should be used discriminatingly. The kind of information that can be elicited by interviewing is not only of observable, objective facts or conditions or events, but also of subjective facts such as

opinions, interpretations, and attitudes of the person interviewed. The objective facts are frequently discoverable by other means, but the subjective facts can be determined only from the individual involved.

When answers to questions can be obtained from records or documents, or by observation of situations, these answers are more reliable, and usually are obtainable more quickly, accurately, and economically than by interviewing. However, even though this is so, you may still want to conduct fact finding interviews. For two reasons: (1) to secure subjective facts, and (2) to secure additional leads that may provide access to more sources of objective data.

b. Appraisal Interview

The appraisal interview is an essential supervisory tool. More and more, supervisors are beginning to realize that "once a year is just not enough." Communication must take place as a continuing day-to-day process.

Real two-way communication between you and the employee cannot possibly be achieved in a mandatory, one-time, annual formal interview. Actually, the number of interviews with any one employee should vary according to individual needs. Whenever you become aware—for example, through an examination of regular work reports, by on-the-job observation, periodic review of work, spot check, etc.—that an employee's performance, good or poor, can profitably be discussed with him, that is the time to talk with him. In other words, the interviews should be carried on naturally, as occasions arise.

This type of interview is used with subordinates to: (1) let them know where they stand, (2) recognize their good work, (3) let them know how, and in what particulars they should improve, (4) develop them in their present jobs, (5) develop and train them for higher jobs, (6) set self-development goals, and (7) to warn borderline employees that they must improve and how.

c. Error Correcting Interview

This type of interview will be a frequent one in your supervisory life. Subordinates like everybody else will make mistakes. Possibly because of personal problems, inaptitude for the job, and even because they haven't been properly trained. Your job in such an interview is to determine the cause of the error so that you can help the subordinate to avoid repeating that error.

d. Grievance Interview

An employee comes to you with a complaint. You interview him to get the facts so that you may either resolve the problem or recommend action to your superiors. This type of interview has always been extremely important and often very difficult. It now has greater implications because of the Government's management-employee cooperation policy. A grievance interview not properly handled could result in magnifying a problem.

e. The Counseling Interview

This interview is intended to help an employee help himself. Counseling is the process of talking things over with an employee who has a problem, in such a way that he will be helped to solve his difficulty and will be better able to cope with difficult situations in the future. Helping the employee solve his problems helps management too get more and better work from the employee.

2. Classified By Method
    a. Individual Interview
        The interviewer and interviewee alone are involved. This type of interview is most frequently used. It can be used for fact finding and grievances and should usually be used in appraisal, error correcting, and counseling interviews.

    b. Group Interview
        One or more interviewers meet with a group of interviewees. This, too, may be used for all types of interviews classified by purpose. It sometimes is more effective than the individual interview. Particularly, if you want to discover leadership ability, ability to get along with others, and problem solving. By presenting a problem for discussion, the interviewer can observe the interaction of the group. Individuals will reveal a great deal of information about themselves by the way they conduct themselves in such a situation.

    c. Panel Interview
        A group or panel of interviewers meet with one interviewee. Here the individual members of the interviewing team have an opportunity to observe and evaluate personal characteristics of the interviewee, his ability to reason, and to express himself clearly, his attitudes, his interests, and what he thinks of his abilities. This type of interview is not used to secure information which can be more accurately secured by other means. For example, IQ can be more accurately determined by appropriate tests. The panel interview is used to measure and evaluate characteristics which are not measurable by other means. As a matter of fact, the less the panel knows about the interviewee's IQ, test scores, educational background, and previous experience, the more valid will be its evaluation.

3. Classified By Technique
    a. Directed
        The directed or controlled interview is used to get facts. It is best described as the question and answer technique. This can be very effective where the interviewee is cooperative, is at ease, and is under no tension or apprehension.

    b. Non-Structured
        A free-flowing interviewing technique used to get information without specifically asking for it. The interviewee is encouraged to talk about whatever it is he wants to talk about. Frequently, this type of interview will get quickly to the core of a problem. The interviewer doesn't have to probe with questions to try to determine what the problem is. This technique is effective in counseling, grievance, and appraisal interviews.

C. How to Conduct Interviews
    1. Preparing for the Interview
        a. Decide your Objective
            What is it that you want to accomplish in the interview? Are you seeking facts? What facts specifically will you need? Are you trying to correct errors, alter behavior, or suggest to the interviewee how he can improve his work? Whatever your objectives, you should have them fixed firmly in your mind. You

might write them down to keep as a ready reference while you conduct the interview. Many interviews fail to accomplish their purpose because the interviewer gets sidetracked from his objectives.

    b. Know the Interviewee

Secure as much information as possible about the person to be interviewed. The more you know about him, the better you will be able to understand his motives, his responses, his frames of reference, and his ability to comprehend.

    c. Make Appointments If At All Possible

Setting aside a definite time to conduct the interview shows the interviewee that you are considerate of his time. You know that the hour is satisfactory to him. By having time allocated in your schedule, you don't waste your time or that of the interviewee.

    d. If Possible, Arrange for Privacy

An interviewee will not be ready to confide in you if he can be overheard by others. Confidential matters or embarrassing facts will be withheld if they are to become public knowledge.

    e. Put Yourself in the Interviewer's Place

Try to take his point of view. How would you feel being interviewed by a person who has your traits, attitudes, and appearance. How would you expect to be treated if you had this or that problem. Having an idea of how the interviewee will react will help you to adjust the manner in which you conduct the interview so that you can accomplish your objectives.

    f. Study Yourself

Try to know your own personality. Each of us is the sum total of his experiences. We have definite attitudes and prejudices. We are not often aware of this, but what we are does affect what we do and how we think. Too often we think in terms of stereotypes. We all know what a "criminal" looks like, don't we? In literature criminals are all shifty-eyed, beetle-browed, and weak-chinned. In real life, contrary to our stereotype image, they frequently have the face of an angel. We should try to know our prejudices, so that even if we can't get rid of them, at least we will not let them intrude in the interview situation.

2. Conducting the Interview
    a. Establish Mutual Confidence

It is the interviewers responsibility to set the tone for the interview. The interviewee must trust you and be willing to confide in you. You have to let him know that you trust him, too. You must show sincerity and must really be sincere. Lack of sincerity is easily spotted and will destroy respect.

    b. Establish Pleasant Associations

There is no need for the interviewer to ever lose his temper. One can be firm without being unpleasant. The interviewee may become angry, and possibly expressing his anger may be helpful, but still the interview should be as pleasant as possible.

c. Put the Interviewee At Ease

He will be more ready to talk if he is relaxed. A good way to put the interviewee at ease is to be at ease yourself. Encourage him to talk by letting him know that you believe his ideas are important and that you are interested in hearing them. Avoid the temptation to evaluate or judge his statements. He should be allowed to express his own ideas, unhampered by your ideas, your values, and preconceptions.

d. Listen to What the Interviewee Says

You are interviewing him to find out what he thinks. You won't find that out listening to your own voice. To be a successful interviewer, one must learn to listen. He must listen not only to the words spoken, but must listen not only to the word spoken, but must listen so that he understands what the interviewee is saying. The interviewee may not be able to express himself clearly, coherently, or logically. The interviewer has to listen attentively to grasp the full meaning of what the interviewee is trying to say.

Listening is extremely important in all interviews, but is particularly important in grievance and counseling interviews. Often times, the mere fact that the interviewee has an attentive interviewer interested in what he is saying is enough to ameliorate the grievance. Just being able to "let off steam" may help the interviewee to see his grievance in better perspective. This is not a newly discovered psychological principle. The Vizier Ptah-Hotep, sometime between 2700 and 2200 B.C. gave this advice to his son: "If thou art one to whom petition is made, be calm as thou listenest to what the petitioner has to say. Do not rebuff him before he has swept out his body or before he has said that for which he came. The petitioner likes attention to his words better than the fulfilling of that for which he came.... It is not necessary that everything about which he has petitioned should come to pass, but a good hearing is soothing to the heart."

e. Allow Enough Time

You can ruin an interview by glancing at your watch. An interviewee is not going to be relaxed and communicative if he has to race the clock. The time allotted should be adequate to accomplish the objectives of the interview. A few minute may be enough to handle some problems, while others may require several hours. Long interviews are exhausting. It is better, where you can, to limit the objectives, and schedule two or more sessions for the interview.

3. Closing the Interview
   a. When to Close

This is not always easy to determine. Circumstances vary both with the type of interview and the personality of the interviewee. With practice, an interviewer can develop an intuition for spotting the appropriate moment for closing the interview. If you have accomplished your interview objectives, or if it becomes apparent that you will not be able to accomplish them, you should bring the interview to a close. If you haven't been able to accomplish your interview objectives, agree on a definite future interview appointment with the interviewee. Nothing is gained by allowing a discussion to drag on. But you should not be abrupt in closing an interview. The interviewee should be assured by your words and manner of your interest and respect.

b. Consolidate Your Gains
Your windup of the interview should be a consolidation of the progress that has been made by the interview: you want the interviewee to leave knowing what has been accomplished. Also, you may avoid future misunderstandings with a good review. Your review should contain these elements:
1. A summary of the points covered
2. A statement of the agreement reached
3. A statement stressing the value of the interview
4. A statement of continuing interest on the part of the interviewer, thus leaving the door open for future interviews.

c. The Natural Closing
The closing of an interview should not be forced. You should not try to end all interviews alike. Be natural. The closing should not be in sharp contrast to the interview. In an interview where you had to admonish an employee, small talk at closing would be inappropriate.

Be sincere in your closing. An incidental "Oh, by the way, how's the family?" said at the door, will mark you as insincere.

A handshake is sometimes appropriate. But if it makes you feel uncomfortable or is inappropriate to the nature of the interview just concluded, then the handshake is out of place. Remember one rule, though, never use a handshake offered you.

D. The Counseling Interview
1. Purpose of Counseling Interview
The primary purpose of counseling is the better adjustment of the employee as a worker, resulting in a more satisfying work experience and increased productivity. Our purpose is to help the employee recognize his limitations, to vocalize his problem, and to assist him in deciding what course of action he can take to improve himself and increase his value to the organization or, sometimes, to accept himself or the situation and to live with it.

We are not trained psychotherapists. If you have any reason to suspect that the individual has a problem with disturbed psychic overtones, don't tamper with the individual. The problems of the human mind, the complexities of neurosis or psychosis are in the province of professional therapists. We have to avoid the temptation to make snap judgments of personality. The layman is eager to identify and categorize. He says, "Joe, you have an inferiority complex." The trained psychologist, social worker, and psychiatrist will study the man intensely before making observations and then won't tell "Joe" about it. Remember, you can cause a lot of damage if you tamper with individuals whose problems are of a complex psychic nature.

2. The Supervisor as a Counselor
As a supervisor, you are the first level of management to receive the impact of problems from your subordinates. Your willingness to listen, your sincere interest in the problems of your employees, and your availability and approachability, will increase your potential as a supervisor.

The supervisor's role as a counselor is one that he cannot avoid, nor should he want to. It gives him an opportunity to learn about his subordinates and what motivates them. It helps him build mutual confidence and respect. It removes barriers to growth. It provides a basis for cooperative effort. It helps to accomplish unit production goals.

E. Interview Checklist

After every interview, you will do well to evaluate yourself as an interviewer. By studying your actions in each interview, you can benefit from your interviewing experience. What did you say or do that contributed to the success of the interview? What did you say or do that caused the interview to be unsuccessful? Your analysis will help to enhance your interviewing skill.

Check yourself against this list.

|     |     | Yes | No |
| --- | --- | --- | --- |
| 1. | Were you friendly? | ☐ | ☐ |
| a. | Did you really feel friendly? | ☐ | ☐ |
| b. | Was this friendliness communicated? | ☐ | ☐ |
| c. | Did the interviewee respond to your friendliness? | ☐ | ☐ |
| 2. | Were you interested in the interviewee as an individual? | ☐ | ☐ |
| 3. | Were you interested in his problem? | ☐ | ☐ |
| 4. | Did you prepare adequately for the interview? | ☐ | ☐ |
| 5. | Did you state your purpose as soon as possible? | ☐ | ☐ |
| 6. | Were you unhurried and relaxed? | ☐ | ☐ |
| 7. | Did the interviewee seem at ease? | ☐ | ☐ |
| 8. | Did you try to reduce his nervousness or fear? | ☐ | ☐ |
| 9. | Did you get him to say what was on his mind? | ☐ | ☐ |
| 10. | Did you give him enough time to talk? | ☐ | ☐ |
| 11. | Did you interrupt his explanations? | ☐ | ☐ |
| 12. | Did you disagree with him? | ☐ | ☐ |
| 13. | If you disagreed, were you pleasant about it? | ☐ | ☐ |
| 14. | Were your questions challenging or argumentative? | ☐ | ☐ |
| 15. | Did you listen to everything he said? | ☐ | ☐ |
| 16. | Was your attitude respectful? | ☐ | ☐ |
| 17. | Did you encourage him to give examples and to elaborate on unclear points? | ☐ | ☐ |
| 18. | Did you invite him to ask questions or raise additional problems? | ☐ | ☐ |
| 19. | Did your gestures help convey your attitude? | ☐ | ☐ |
| 20. | Did you refrain from giving advice or lecturing? | ☐ | ☐ |
| 21. | Did you make any reference to your continued interest and willingness to help? | ☐ | ☐ |
| 22. | Did you answer his questions? | ☐ | ☐ |
| 23. | Did you summarize the gains made? | ☐ | ☐ |
| 24. | Did you close on a friendly note? | ☐ | ☐ |
| 25. | Do you have a plan for following-up the interview? | ☐ | ☐ |

### III. SUMMARY

We have discussed the nature of interviewing and have seen that it is an art in which you can become skilled. We have discussed the various types of interview and have classified them by purpose, method, and technique.

We have discussed how interviews should be conducted. We stressed the importance of preparing for an interview, suggested steps to follow in conducting the interview, and analyzed the closing of the interview. Together, we looked at the nature of the counseling interview and saw that, for our purposes, it concerns normal problems of normal people. We saw that the sole objective of the counseling interview is to lead the interview to a clear understanding of his problem so that he realizes what action to take and assumes responsibility for taking it.

We then reviewed a checklist that you may use to evaluate your interviewing ability. Remember, how successful an interviewer you become depends entirely on you.

## INTERVIEWING AND COUNSELING
## SAMPLE QUESTIONS

1. Question: What are the purposes of interviews?
   Answer: To obtain information, to give information, to solve problems, to influence behavior.

2. Question: How does a panel interview differ from a group interview?
   Answer: A panel interview: More than one interviewer, only one interviewee.
   A group interview: One or more interviewers, and more than one interviewee.

3. Question: When is a directed interview effective?
   Answer: When the interviewee is cooperative, is relaxed, and is under no tension or apprehension.

4. Question: What is the non-structured approach?
   Answer: It is a free-flowing interviewing technique in which the interviewee is encouraged to talk about what he wants to.

5. Question: How should you prepare for an interview?
   Answer: Determine your objectives, know the interviewee, make a definite appointment, arrange for privacy, put yourself in interviewee's place, study yourself.

6. Question: What should you remember in conducting an interview?
   Answer: To establish mutual confidence, to establish pleasant associations, to put the interviewee at ease, to listen, and to allow enough time.

7. Question: How should you close the interview?
   Answer: Close at the appropriate point, consolidate your gains, and use a natural closing.

8. Question: How does counseling help the employee?
   Answer: Helps employee understand the obstacles to his future growth and development, helps employee to recognize his limitations, helps him vocalize his problems, assists him in solving his problems.

9. Question: How does counseling help the supervisor?
   Answer: It gives him opportunity to learn what motivates his subordinates, it helps build mutual confidence and respect, releases potential of employees, improves cooperation, and helps achieve production goals.

## INTERVIEWING AND COUNSELING
## OUTLINE 1

**Interviews—Classified by Purpose**
    Fact-Finding Interviews
    —To secure subjective facts
    —To secure additional leads that may provide access to more sources of objective data
    Appraisal Interview
    —To let employee know where he stands
    —To recognize good work
    —To let employee know how, and in what particulars, he should improve
    —To develop employees in present jobs
    —To develop and train them for higher jobs
    —To set self-development goals
    —To warn borderline employees that they must improve and how
    Error Correcting Interview
    —To determine cause of errors
    —To help employee to avoid repetition of errors
    Grievance Interview
    —To afford aggrieved employee opportunity to be heard
    —To collect information
    —To act on grievance either directly or by recommending action to your superiors
    Counseling Interview
    —To help employee solve his personal problems
    —To improve morale
    —To improve production
    —To improve work habits

## INTERVIEWING AND COUNSELING
## OUTLINE 2

**Interviews—Classified By Method**
    Individual Interview
    —One interviewer and one interviewee alone are involved
    —Used for fact-finding, appraisal, error correcting, grievances, and counseling
    Group Interview
    —One or more interviewers meet with a group of interviewees
    —Useful in observing individual reactions in a group situation. Exposes leadership ability, ability to get along with others, and ability to solve problems
    Panel Interview
    —A group or panel of interviewers meet with one interviewee
    —Used to observe and evaluate personal characteristics of interviewee, his ability to reason and express himself clearly, his attitudes, his interests, and what he thinks of his abilities

**Interviews—Classified by Technique**
    Directed Interview
    —Used to get facts
    —Direct questioning is used
    —Is effective where interviewee is cooperative, relaxed, and is under no tension or apprehension
    Non-structured Interview
    —Free-flowing technique used to get information without specifically asking for it
    —Interviewee is encouraged to talk about whatever he wants to talk about
    —The interviewer does not probe—he listens
    —This technique is effective in counseling, grievances and appraisal interviews

## INTERVIEWING AND COUNSELING
## OUTLINE 3

**How to Conduct Interviews**
    Preparing for the Interview
        a. Decide what the objective or objectives of this interview will be
        b. Know the interviewer
        c. Make a definite appointment for the interview
        d. Arrange for a place of privacy to conduct the interview
        e. Put yourself in the interviewee's place
        f. Study yourself
    Conducting the interview
        a. Establish mutual confidence
        b. Establish pleasant associations
        c. Put the interviewee at ease
        d. Listen to what the interviewee says
        e. Allow enough time
    Closing the Interview
        a. Close at the appropriate point. Don't cut interview short—don't drag it out
        b. Consolidate your gains by:
            —Summarizing the points covered
            —Restating the agreements reached
            —Stressing the value of this interview
            —Expressing continued interest and leaving the door open for future interview
        c  The natural closing
            —Don't force it
            —Be natural
            —Be sincere

## 13

## INTERVIEWING AND COUNSELING
## OUTLINE 4

**The Counseling Interview**
    Purpose of Counseling Interview
    —To help the employee understand the obstacles to further growth and development that are typified by his specific difficulty
    —To help the employee to recognize his limitations
    —To help him vocalize his problems
    —To assist him in deciding what course of action to take
    —To deal with the normal problems of normal people
    The Supervisor as a Counselor
    —A role you cannot avoid, nor should you want to
    —You learn what motivates your subordinates
    —You build mutual confidence and respect
    —You remove barriers to growth
    —You improve cooperation
    —You increase probability of accomplishing unit production goals

## INTERVIEWING AND COUNSELING
## OUTLINE 5
## INTERVIEW CHECKLIST

|     |                                                                              | Yes | No |
|-----|------------------------------------------------------------------------------|-----|-----|
| 1.  | Were you friendly?                                                           | ☐ | ☐ |
|     | a. Did you really feel friendly?                                             | ☐ | ☐ |
|     | b. Was this friendliness communicated?                                       | ☐ | ☐ |
|     | c. Did the interviewee respond to our friendliness?                          | ☐ | ☐ |
| 2.  | Were you interested in the interviewee as an individual?                     | ☐ | ☐ |
| 3.  | Were you interested in his problem?                                          | ☐ | ☐ |
| 4.  | Did you prepare adequately for the interview?                                | ☐ | ☐ |
| 5.  | Did you state your purpose as soon as possible?                              | ☐ | ☐ |
| 6.  | Were you unhurried and relaxed?                                              | ☐ | ☐ |
| 7.  | Did the interviewee seem at ease?                                            | ☐ | ☐ |
| 8.  | Did you try to reduce his nervousness or fear?                               | ☐ | ☐ |
| 9.  | Did you get him to say what was on his mind?                                 | ☐ | ☐ |
| 10. | Did you give him enough time to talk?                                        | ☐ | ☐ |
| 11. | Did you interrupt his explanations?                                          | ☐ | ☐ |
| 12. | Did you disagree with him?                                                   | ☐ | ☐ |
| 13. | If you disagreed, were you pleasant about it?                                | ☐ | ☐ |
| 14. | Were your questions challenging our argumentative?                           | ☐ | ☐ |
| 15. | Did you listen to everything he said?                                        | ☐ | ☐ |
| 16. | Was your attitude respectful?                                                | ☐ | ☐ |
| 17. | Did you encourage him to give examples and to elaborate on unclear points?   | ☐ | ☐ |
| 18. | Did you invite him to ask questions or raise additional problems?            | ☐ | ☐ |
| 19. | Did your gestures help convey your attitude?                                 | ☐ | ☐ |
| 20. | Did you refrain from giving advice or lecturing?                             | ☐ | ☐ |
| 21. | Did you make any reference to your continued interest and willingness to help? | ☐ | ☐ |
| 22. | Did you answer his questions?                                                | ☐ | ☐ |
| 23. | Did you summarize the gains made?                                            | ☐ | ☐ |
| 24. | Did you close on a friendly note?                                            | ☐ | ☐ |
| 25. | Do you have a plan for following-up the interview?                           | ☐ | ☐ |

www.ingramcontent.com/pod-product-compliance
Lightning Source LLC
Chambersburg PA
CBHW082127230426

43671CB00015B/2827